SINGING GOD'S WORK

*The Inspirational Music, People and Stories
of the Harlem Gospel Choir*

**Allen Bailey
with Penelope Holt**

YORK HOUSE PRESS

Copyright © 2009 by Allen Bailey with Penelope Holt

York House Press.   All rights reserved.
No part of this book may be copied, scanned, reproduced or distributed in print or digitally without express permission by the publisher.

York House Press
800 Westchester Avenue, Suite 641 North
Rye Brook, NY 10573

ISBN 13: 978-0-9791956-5-5, York House Press
First edition, October, 2009
Library of Congress number: 2009936544

Cover design by Concise Marketing & Communications

Dedicated to the memory of my wonderful and loving parents, George Bailey and Rose Lee Bailey, who taught me that the greatest gift of all is giving.

To all our fans, I hope that this book gives you a better understanding of the Harlem Gospel Choir, its mission, its music, its ministry, its joyful noise.

Acknowledgements

There is a lifetime's worth of people whom I would like to thank for providing and enriching the experiences that I write about. I would like to thank Dick and Penny for their enthusiasm for my story and their faith in my ability to tell it. Thank you to Doug Kenyon at Hunton and Williams for all his help in making this book happen. Thank you to Bob Hardcastle for his invaluable advice, which helps to keep the ministry afloat in rough financial seas. Thanks and praise for the late Reverend Preston Washington of Memorial Baptist Church, Harlem, for his abiding support and friendship; for Reverend Rene Washington, senior pastor at Memorial Baptist Church, Harlem, for her enduring kindness; for Deacon Ford, Memorial Baptist Church, Harlem, for unending knowledge and humor.

My love and thanks to all the members of the Choir, present and past, for their faith, joy and God-given talents; to Terri and John Traverso for sharing our vision and running with it; to Nigel Hassler of Helter Skelter, England; to Rita Zappador of International Music, Italy; to Milena Paleckova of 10:15 Agency, Czech Republic; to Giedrius Klimasauskas of MakroConcerts, Lithuania; to Darryl Downey of Raglane Entertainment, Ireland; to all our friends at East Coast Entertainment; to our agents and promoters around the world who continue to believe in our ministry; and to William Lobelson at Germain and Maureau who protects our trademark with a sword of fire.

Allen and Penelope both wish to thank Anna Bailey and Kia Raf for their keen storytelling ability, their hours of work and their help in preparing this manuscript.

Author Bios

Allen Bailey has lived on Manhattan all his life and still loves to return to his roots in Harlem even after a short time away from New York. He lives with Anna, his wife of twenty-one years, and their dog Max. Together they manage and tour year round with the world famous Harlem Gospel Choir.

Penelope Holt lives in Westchester, New York. She is the author of *The Apple: Based on the Herman Rosenblat Holocaust Love Story*, 2009, and *The Painter's Gift*, 2007.

Table of Contents

   I. Election Night in Times Square 1
  II. Harlem Days 6
 III. Black Church: Home Away from Home 16
  IV. A Divine Birthday 19
   V. At the Knee of Comedy Great, Pigmeat Markham 25
  VI. Basketball and Music 30
 VII. In the Company of Legends:
       Miles Davis and Nina Simone 37
VIII. The Motown Years 44
 VIV. Dr. King and the March on Washington 50
   X. A Very Big Man: Kareem Abdul-Jabbar 54
  XI. Changing the World 58
 XII. The Commodores Years 63
XIII. The Birth of the Harlem Gospel Choir 68
 XIV. How the Other Half Lives 84
  XV. America's Own Paul Newman 88
 XVI. Rumble in the Jungle: Ali Versus Foreman.....................92
XVII. A Mighty Talent: Performers of the Choir 101
XVIII. The Power of Gospel Music 109
 XIV. On the Road Again 120
  XX. The Flying Dutchman: André Rieu............................... 134
 XXI. The Queen of Daytime TV and Rock Royalty:
       Oprah and Lisa Marie Presley......................... 139
XXII. A Oneness Heart: Sri Chinmoy 143
XXIII. Two Popes and a President............................... 147
XXIV. Sundays at Home in New York 154
 XXV. Farewell to Michael Jackson............................ 158

One

Election Night in Times Square

"I enclose a copy of my song, 'Obama', written in tribute for your new President. I think it would be ideal for your renowned choir."
—Steve, Merseyside, England

It is November 4, 2008, election night in America. My wife, Anna, and my niece, Kia, are mingling with other guests in a party atmosphere, at the BBC's Election Night Broadcast at the Marriott Renaissance Hotel, overlooking Times Square, in New York City. They are at the party to represent the Harlem Gospel Choir, and me, its founder and director. I'm unable to attend this special event, because I am on tour with the Choir in the Czech Republic. Thousands of miles away, in a different time zone, I am tired, but wide-awake and nervous, as I monitor the election night results, watching what I pray will be a history-making night unfold.

The BBC's invitation to its election night soiree had come unexpectedly, weeks before, and left me feeling flattered and honored. It described the event as "a small gathering of the great and the good; some of New York's movers and shakers; people from all walks of life, who reflect the diversity of the great city. People, also, who will be brilliant speakers on air, telling a global audience of millions what the election results mean for them and their sectors or areas of life."

The invitation, which came via email, was such a surprise, and so exciting, that I told Anna to keep it, because I had the vague notion that I might want to frame it one day. Even more overwhelming was what the invitation went on to say: "It would be particularly interesting to hear from you, given your background as a giant in the entertainment industry, who has always contributed significantly to the community around you. As founder of the Harlem Gospel Choir, we would welcome your spiritual company, on such an historic night. The Harlem Gospel Choir is one of the great attractions of New York, worldwide, and it would be an honour (sic) to share your company." I admit that I had to read this part through a couple of times, just to make sure that they were actually referring to me, and had not sent it to me by mistake.

This election night is indeed historic, and one that the BBC and media outlets in America, and beyond, want to capture in its every shade and nuance. For me, an African-American man, who grew up in a rat-infested tenement in Harlem, the night is more, it is transcendent; a milestone in my community and in my personal history that I had always hoped would come, but feared would not.

As my wife and niece mingle at the BBC party with the "movers and shakers," among whose numbers I have apparently been counted, I lie on a bed in my hotel room. I don't feel like a "mover and shaker." I feel like a humble man, giving thanks that a cornerstone of Dr. King's Dream just might come true in its most sublime form. On this night, there is a good chance that a black man, Barack Hussein Obama, judged not by the color of his skin, but by the content of his character, will be elected as the forty-fourth president of the United States.

In the darkened room with the TV flickering, I watch, as back home, the votes come in, state by state. I have had, as the saying goes, a front-row seat to history, and have participated in many of the major milestones of the last sixty years in African-American culture: I experienced Dr. King's ministry firsthand, and I was inspired, by Dr. King's vision of nation building and service, to become a community organizer myself. I participated in the Civil Rights Movement and marched with thousands on Washington to hear Reverend King's most memorable speech, when he told the world, "I Have a Dream." And later, gutted by Dr. King's assassination, I was moved to join with others to work for the creation of a national holiday to celebrate his birthday, every year on January 15.

But, perhaps my most radically positive act in response to Dr. King's legacy, was to found the Harlem Gospel Choir, an idea that came on the very first national holiday celebrating Dr. King's birthday, on Martin Luther King Jr. Day, 1986. In the twenty-three years since then, I have logged more than two million touring miles with the Choir, sharing with audiences around the world, the richness of the African-American culture, and the unique flavor of Harlem.

Let me say it, right here, that the Harlem Gospel Choir is, first and foremost, a touring ministry that ministers through music, and uses music to raise money for children around the globe. And what can I say about the music from this mighty Choir? It is a foot-tapping, soul-swelling, spirit-raising, roof-lifting and joyful noise that makes people, worldwide, feel inspired and uplifted, reminding them why life is worth living, and why community is so important.

On election night, 2008, as I watch the BBC broadcast on TV and see the crowds swelling on Broadway, most of them waiting and hoping for the same outcome as I am, I keep thinking back to my mother and her daily struggles in Harlem, with six sons and one daughter.

By around 11:00 PM U.S. Eastern time, the race is over, and what I had always thought impossible, is made manifest: Barack Obama becomes president-elect of the United States of America, ushering in the collective hope that his term in office will bring the best for all Americans, and for the world. I watch as a huge roar erupts from the crowd in Times Square.

The BBC continues coverage from its perch in the Renaissance, and I look at the TV, squinting to find Anna and Kia among the partygoers. Finally, I watch as my niece, Kia, is interviewed on camera; a beautiful, poised, young black woman, she is expressing what now President-Elect Obama means to her generation. I see that people can't stop cheering, and many, like me, who thought that this day would never come, are crying and hugging each other in hope and amazement; friends and strangers alike, they are all friends tonight.

Still later, I watch Barack Obama's victory speech from Chicago. I think back to the Democratic National Convention, just two months earlier, when I had listened to Barack's acceptance speech after he had received his party's nomination. Tonight, as on that night, I can see Dr. King's spirit in the young man who will soon be president, and I realize that I am experiencing the second of two major addresses by a black man to the American nation.

Back in 1963, Dr. King addressed a massive crowd that had marched on Washington, demanding civil rights and equality. Now, forty-five years later in Chicago, Barack Obama accepts the presidency. It has been only eight months since the Harlem Gospel Choir performed for him at the Apollo Theater, back in February 2008, during primary season.

When I met Barack Obama at the Apollo, on that evening in Harlem, the then senator from Illinois immediately impressed me, because he was very sincere. He said how much he was looking forward to the concert. When he had heard that the event coordinator, New York State Senator, Bill Perkins, had booked the Choir to perform, he was excited, he said, because he had been a fan for many years.

I took the liberty of telling Barack that I was impressed with him from the standpoint of an athlete. Both he and I played basketball in college, and I mentioned that I had recently watched a film clip of him playing. He had missed a lay-up, and gone back for the rebound, went up again, missed it again, and then went back up again, against guys as big as trees.

Although he missed, I saw that Barack, the shorter, skinnier guy, kept going back. Because of this, I told him that I could relate to him as someone who understood what it took to get things done. He was obviously very determined. He had been through a lot of troubles, as I had, and knew what it was to have to keep going.

"I bet you thought the day of fighting the big guys for rebounds was over," I said. The senator laughed and told me that his right-hand man on the campaign, Jerry, used to play ball at Duke University, and that every morning they had a pick-up game of basketball, before the business of the day got underway. "That's great," I said, "that you can take time out to do something you so obviously enjoy."

I also remarked that I thought his wife would be a terrific role model for black women in the United States, looking to be inspired by a prominent African-American woman. For years, I had toured as an advance man for the Commodores, and Michelle Obama often made me think me of the group's big hit: "You're Once, Twice, Three Times a Lady."

"I think Mrs. Obama will be a great First Lady," I said, "well received throughout the world, and well respected throughout the United States."

After the photo shoot that evening at the Apollo, Barack promised that we would see him again really soon, probably at the inauguration at the White House. I yelled out that I would hold him to that, and we just laughed, because it seemed like a great idea, but an improbable one—to me at least.

As I watch election night in New York, what seemed improbable—the confirming of Barack Obama as president-elect—is real. It makes me think back on my own American journey, also improbable, but nonetheless real. Times Square at Forty-second Street and Broadway is less than a hundred blocks from Harlem, but a million miles away from my humble beginnings, there.

Two

Harlem Days

"Thank you for taking us to Harlem to experience the Black Church and to be touched by Jesus. Bless you for traveling all this way."
–Libby, Australia

I was born in Harlem Hospital, on September 2, 1940, back when Harlem was a poor, but nevertheless, extremely vibrant community. I was the second youngest child of six siblings—five brothers and one sister. My older brothers were John; David, who always went by the name Tracy; and Curtis, who is just one year older than I. My sister's name was Dorothy, Dot for short. Dot was already ten years old when I was born. My younger brother's name was George, after our father, but we always called him Bab'Brother. He accepted this nickname all his life, but complained very vocally, if anyone ever mistakenly called him Baby Brother. Today, only Curtis and I are still in the land of the living.

Our childhood was spent in Central Harlem. We lived in a cold-water flat in a dilapidated brown tenement. It was a roach-infested walk-up on West 134th Street, between Lenox Avenue and Fifth Avenue. Our apartment had no hot running water, and there was no air conditioning in summer, and no heat in winter.

In summer, we would all sit on the stoop, trying to catch a cool breeze. Many of the older folk in the building brought out chairs to sit on the sidewalk, listening to music, usually jazz, which played on some radio that sat in the window of one of the apartments facing the street. They would talk about this and that, trying to figure out how to make their lives a little easier, and enjoying the street vibe. Come winter, we boiled water on the stove for bathing, and tried to heat up the freezing apartment.

One of my first memories of living in that apartment, is of being bitten on the face by a rat, when I was about six years old. My mother used to set rat traps around the house, using cheese as bait, but during that time, we were so often hungry, that I had learned how to remove the cheese from a trap without setting it off. But the rats were as hungry as we were, and the night that the rat bit me, it had no doubt been attracted to my bed by the smell of cheese that I had stolen from the traps.

Lying in my bed, late at night, I could hear the rats moving around inside the walls of the apartment. My friend, Benny Bay, who lived next door to us, decided to do something about them, because his apartment had an even bigger rat infestation than ours did. One day, he brought home a street cat in the mistaken belief that it would catch the rats and solve the problem. The next day, Benny found the cat lying dead on the floor of his bedroom; the rats had killed it.

Besides the rats, our day-to-day living conditions were often hazardous to our health. One day, Mom kept me off school, which naturally made me happy, because the ceiling had collapsed while I was in bed, and falling plaster had hit me on the head. It had been raining heavily, and we lived on the top floor of this five-story walk-up. I guess the roof had been leaking for a while, saturating the plaster, until eventually it separated from the ceiling, and fell down on my head as I slept. The superintendent came up and put cardboard over the ceiling to cover the hole. I remember lying in bed, looking up at the cardboard, taped across the ceiling. That was a very cold, wet and miserable winter.

Today, our old building is no longer there. It was torn down in the mid-1950s and replaced by a development called Lenox Terrace. The new tenants were black urban professionals and entertainers. Some of its more famous current residents include Percy Sutton, who was Malcolm X's lawyer, and one of the coordinators of the Martin Luther King March on Washington, in 1964; and Congressman, Charles Rangel, who keeps an apartment there. A good friend of mine, James Ford, who is a deacon at Memorial Baptist Church, also lives there. And one of our tour managers, Henry, moved into Lenox Terrace earlier this year. He says that he would rather live in

Park Slope, Brooklyn, but I think that after a few more months, he will really begin to enjoy the vibrancy of the neighborhood, and the advantages of its central location. Lenox Terrace is the complete opposite of my first childhood home.

We lived at 24 West 134th Street until I was about thirteen years old. Finally, the housing application that my mother had submitted to the city housing authority was approved, and we were allocated a three-bedroom apartment in a brand new housing project, located at the corner of 134th Street and Madison Avenue. Members of my family still live there today.

The day that we moved to the projects was a great day in our lives, and I remember that our neighbors were very envious of us, as we closed the door to that old flat for the last time. Our new address was 2144 Madison Avenue, Apartment 3A, Abraham Lincoln Houses (Lincoln Projects for short). It was subsidized city housing, but it was new and clean with hot running water, and even an elevator.

The grounds had gardens, walkways and a playground. For us, it was luxury, and my brothers and I were fascinated with everything, especially the elevator. Like most of the other kids in the building, we had no appreciation of nice things, because we had never had nice things. We loved to ride up and down in the elevator, from the first floor to the sixth floor, trying to get it to stop in between the floors. We constantly broke this new plaything and then we had to walk upstairs. Luckily for us, our apartment was only on the third floor.

My first memories of school are from my days at PS 133 at Fifth Avenue and East 131st Street. All my life, I have had poor penmanship, and I think it's because the usual punishment for talking in class, or not doing your homework, was to write lines on the blackboard after school. After writing "I must not talk in class" fifty times on the board, I would resort to scribbling the words as fast as I could, so I might get out of the room and go play with my friends, who were in detention like me, or waiting outside to play.

Our favorite game was basketball, which we played in the school playground after school and on weekends. I was a forward and I loved the game that kept me so busy. Our school was brand new, and it had a gymnasium, unlike most of the other older schools in the area. Sometimes, basketball tournaments between neighborhood schools were held in our gymnasium, but my parents could seldom attend, they were too busy working or looking for work.

If I was not playing basketball, I was playing stickball in the street. I played first base, and took my job very seriously, guarding the sewer cover, or a beat-up garbage can cover, that acted as the base. One time, I was so intent on trying to catch the ball that I didn't see the taxi coming right at me. It hit me, as it went by, knocking me over a parked car. Friends rushed me over to Harlem Hospital with cuts on my arms and legs, but no broken bones, thankfully. Our next-door neighbor called a lawyer for us, and we settled with the taxicab company for a small sum of money, because the driver had been driving above the speed limit. But, as so often happens with these kinds of cases, the lawyer pocketed most of the money.

Junior high days were spent at PS 89 at 139th Street and Lenox Avenue. In those days, the city junior high schools provided breakfast and lunch, but unlike in the elementary schools, these meals were not free. My mother would have had to pay one or two dollars, per week, per child, so that we could get cheese, an apple and milk for breakfast, and she just couldn't afford it. One of the most humiliating things for us poor kids was to be put in a separate room, because we did not have meal tickets for breakfast or lunch.

At lunchtime, we would skip out of school or play basketball, but this was not an option early in the morning, when other kids made fun of us, because we could not afford the meal tickets. Eventually, to avoid the embarrassment, I started arriving at school after the breakfast, but this led to a string of late notices being sent home. The teachers wanted to expel me, but my mother understood my predicament, and she came down to the school to defend me, every time the guidance counselor contacted her. The school said that I was too fidgety, that I did not pay attention, and kept getting out of my seat. "There is nothing wrong with him," my mother explained to the teachers, "except that he had no breakfast this morning and no dinner last night. You'd fidget if you were as hungry as he is."

My mother, Rose Lee, came from Ebensburg, Pennsylvania. She was a tiny woman, only four feet eleven; quiet, dignified and religious, and she loved church. Unlike most of the ladies I knew, my mom had straight hair and a straight nose, because she was part Native American; her skin was olive and her eyes were hazel.

Like almost everybody else in the neighborhood, my family was poor with a capital P. Even though we lived in subsidized housing and received welfare, there were six children, and the welfare check was not sufficient, even when they added food stamps to it. To feed us, my mom found work as a domestic, and she was paid in cash, "off the books." She would ride the bus or subway downtown to Greenwich Village to clean white people's houses. She always dressed like a lady and never wore slacks, and when she went off to clean, she wore the maid's uniform that the rich white families she worked for had given her.

Mom worked hard, down on her knees, scrubbing floors, cleaning all the edges, all the nooks and crannies, with an old toothbrush and a cup of bleach. She was extremely fastidious, and in demand with her employers, because she was so thorough. Unexpectedly, she might sometimes ask to inspect the gentleman of the house to see if he had a ring around the collar. If he did, she ordered him to take off his shirt so she could put it in the cleaners, whether he thought it needed a wash or not.

My mother had an interesting way of selecting the people she would work for: she inspected their bathrooms. Mom thought that a person's bathroom held the key to their character. She turned down plenty of work from rich people because their bathroom didn't pass inspection. "Allen, if people don't have respect for their own personal hygiene, how do you think they are going to treat you?" she used to tell me. My mother had only a third-grade education, but she had the intelligence that came from studying what she called the book of common sense.

"Cleanliness is next to godliness," she told us boys, and for us, being clean was essential. Mom would line us up to look at our necks and down our ears, and then scrub us with a wire brush, if we didn't pass inspection. We hollered, because it was just torture. "I do not care if you have only one pair of underwear," Mom lectured us, "every night you wash them and put them in the oven to dry. People might talk about us because we are poor, but don't you ever let them talk about you because you are not clean." She made sure that the five Bailey boys were always well mannered and scrupulously clean.

Mom also taught us boys to cook and clean. "You'd better learn," she said, "because there is no guarantee that some woman is gonna do it for you."

She gave us all jobs and mine was the laundry. From the time that I was six or seven years old, I did the laundry for all seven people in my family. Mom showed me how to work the machines at the laundry in our project, how to use bleach and detergent to make the clothes clean and fresh smelling, and how to fold the clothes. Later, I taught my brothers, and then they taught their children, so all the Bailey kids are experts when it comes to laundry. Even now, my wife, Anna, invites me do the laundry on a regular basis.

Dad was the complete opposite of my Mom: six foot three inches tall and very good looking. His friends in the projects called him Big George Bailey. He loved a good time and nursed dreams of being a professional entertainer.

Back when Dad was young, in the 1940s, jitterbugging was a very popular dance, and Dad was ready for anything after a hard day's work on the docks. He loved to dress up in the crazy-colored Zoot suits that were all the rage. My mother refused to go out dancing with him because she said he looked foolish, and on most Friday nights when Dad got paid, there was an argument. Mom wanted him to stay home and save money to pay bills, but Dad was always itching to go party at the Savoy, the top spot for dances, and to hang out with his buddies. The neighborhood guys thought they were very smooth. Cool, calm and collected, they knew how to get the ladies, and how to treat them. It was a time, I recall, when men were very respectful of women, and very mannerly.

Dad tried his hand at Vaudeville a couple of times. He tap danced and told corny jokes, convinced that he could get rich at it, like Buck and Bubbles, a popular dance team at the time, but it didn't pan out. Dad couldn't make money as an entertainer, and my mother hated all that "stuff and nonsense," as she called it. "You're already a fool; why look like a bigger fool?" she used to tell him. Tough words, but Mom had her feet on the ground and a family to feed. I remember Mom and Dad arguing, because money was short, and because she wanted him to give up clowning around, but other than this kind of bickering, I never really heard either of them complain.

As much as it was exciting to move to the projects, it was also a sad time, because our father was prohibited from moving there with us. The law at the time stipulated that if a family received any welfare or subsidized housing from the city, then there could be no able-bodied men of income-earning age in the home. We called this law "the slave law," because it broke up so many families, just like slavery did. Able-bodied men—husbands and fathers, who were able to get work, were not allowed to live with their families in subsidized housing. It made no sense to us. It still makes no sense to me, and, if I'm right, this law was not abolished until the 1990s. So that was that; my father could not come, and instead, he had to find a room at the YMCA.

Dad had a little job loading and unloading trucks in the garment center. He visited us when he could, and brought some of his wages to help Mom feed us, but he had to be careful, because had he been caught helping us, we would have lost the apartment. The social workers paid neighbors, willing to report those husbands who were sneaking in. Fortunately, my father never got caught, but many of our friends who lived in the projects, lost their apartments, because their fathers were caught coming by, trying to help support their families.

As the family grew yet bigger with the arrival of Bab'Brother, Dad gave up his dreams of Vaudeville, and more and more, got into working as a longshoreman. It was hard physical labor. Often, he didn't get a wage, as such, just money paid in hand for a few days of work, unloading the big ships that came into the seaports, up and down the East Coast.

Out-and-out racism was alive and well, of course. White workers were hired first, and then, whatever was left over would go to the black guys, and those jobs were the hardest and dirtiest. My dad and his friends toiled out in the bitter cold for eight or nine hours at a stretch, eating lunch as they worked. Dad came home with his hands and feet frozen, but he never complained, because he had seven mouths to feed.

When work dried up in New York City, Dad went on the road, traveling as far down the coast as Philadelphia to find day work. It was grueling, but I think he loved working outside, laughing and joking with his buddies. But, even with Mom making a little extra as a scrub, Dad still couldn't earn enough to keep the family going, which meant that eventually my mother had to go on welfare.

So, over time, even though my parents had a good relationship, Dad's not living with us tore the marriage apart. He tried to come and visit, but I remember my mom experienced a lot of paranoia, because of those welfare spies, who earned a little extra in their welfare checks for snitching on their neighbors. My parents were both working hard, but there was not enough money coming in, and the price they paid for needing welfare was a broken marriage. It was a crazy system that tore families apart and created more poverty than it cured.

Like so many poor folks do, my mother bought on credit from the milkman and other trades-people, and she could never get out of the debt, because they charged such a high rate of interest. The welfare check would come in, but by the time Mom had paid what she owed with interest, and bought some food essentials, she was back in a financial hole.

My mom was one of the hardest-working people I ever met, volunteering when she could in church, raising five boys, and working as a scrub. Sometimes, she dragged herself home from work, bringing back scraps from her employer's table. She even salvaged food that someone had bit into; you could see the teeth marks in the leftover bread or meat she gave us. It drove my oldest brother, Tracy, just crazy to see that bread with a bite out of it. "I ain't eating it," he used to shout. "Bread is bread," my mother would answer with a shrug.

After junior high school, I enrolled in the High School of Fashion Industries, on West Twenty-fourth Street and Seventh Avenue. I had always been interested in fashion, and whenever I could, I saved my money to buy *Town & Country* or *Menswear Magazine*. I stared at the pictures and thought about how fantastic it would be to dress in designer clothes, and go to dinner at fashionable restaurants.

I hid the magazines from my friends, so they wouldn't laugh at me for being a dreamer, who, never in a million years, could afford such a gracious lifestyle. At the time, I might have agreed with them, but that didn't stop me from dreaming, and looking for ways to earn a little extra cash.

Back then, Brooklyn's projects were controlled by gangs, such as the Sportsmen and El Quentos that lived in the housing projects in Bedford Stuyvesant, Brownsville and Williamsburg. Milk and dairy products were still delivered door to door by milkmen, who feared the gangs, and were often reluctant to come into the black neighborhoods and projects.

The gang leader of the Sportsmen, a guy called Sammy, was in my class at Fashion Industries. One day, he found himself in a quandary: his grandmother had not received her milk that day, because his own gang had stopped white milkmen from delivering to his grandmother's building in Bedford Stuyvesant.

I suggested to Sammy that he organize protection for the milkmen, who could pay the gang, out of their own pockets, to deliver the milk for them. Really it was a form of extortion, but the milkmen were happy, because their work was being done for them, and they could call their supervisors each day to report that all the milk deliveries had been made; the residents were happy, because they were getting their milk delivered; and Sammy and the Sportsmen were happy, because they were getting paid, while still maintaining their gang identities. I was happy too, because Sammy used to tip me and take me to lunch. Pretty soon, I joined the racket, and we got very busy, protecting as many as five milk vans at a time, and earning big money, because the milkmen were each willing to fork out between twenty-five and fifty bucks, per night, to get the job done.

One night I went with Sammy to help with the milk deliveries. I remember all the stops we made in each building, hiking up to the fifteenth floor of one apartment building, because the elevator was broken, then coming all the way back down, floor by floor, trying to remember which apartments had ordered milk, and how many bottles.

By the time I was done with my shift, that night, it was time for school. I always made sure to dress so that I could go right to school from work. I don't think my mother ever knew about this little enterprise, and I used the money Sammy tipped me to buy food after school, or to go to the movies.

As I branched out into doing more odd jobs, I started turning most of what I earned, over to my mother. She kept what little money she had in an old oatmeal box on top of the cupboard, and the most heartbreaking thing was to witness my oldest brother, Tracy, after he got into drugs, start stealing that hard-earned cash.

Tracy held a close resemblance to our father, George, and, like George, he was very lovable, very tall and very good-looking. He loved to talk and laugh, and he had a bad habit of talking with food in his mouth, but unlike Dad, there was a very destructive side to Tracy's personality. Out on the street, he could be a bully, who threatened to break your head, because he thought that was how to earn respect in the neighborhood.

It was around age fourteen that Tracy started using heroin, and stealing money from the oatmeal box that we were all working so hard to fill. My poor mother was beside herself, as she peered through the keyhole of Tracy's bedroom, to behold the sad sight of him and his friends shooting up. To discourage his habit, she took the lock off his door, but it didn't deter him. I used to peek through the keyhole, too, and the sight of my wonderful big brother sticking a needle into his arm, was terrible to me. He had turned his room into a shooting gallery and I just did not know what to say to him.

As the drugs took hold of Tracy, the money in the oatmeal box was not enough to feed his habit, and he began robbing people in the street and the subway. His friends told us what Tracy was doing to get easy cash, but no amount of talking from us could change the direction he had chosen for his life.

Over the next few years, Tracy went to jail several times for drug use and robbery. We boys went with Mom to visit our brother when we could, and those were very sad days. Eventually, as he became more hard-bitten, Tracy wound up killing a couple of people in jail, but he didn't start out that way; he wasn't always on drugs.

Tracy had a sweet nature and a beautiful smile, and he was very bright. At one point, he was in charge of protecting our neighborhood, and he looked out for the girls as they walked through the grounds of the projects, chasing off the guys from neighboring projects who tried to menace them.

Everyone in the neighborhood liked Tracy, until he started going downhill, and getting mean and callous because of the drugs. One day, his body was discovered in an abandoned building in Harlem. He had died from a heroin overdose. I loved Tracy, and his death is one of the big regrets of my life. What would have happened if I could have gotten closer to him and done more for him? It's a question that still haunts me.

Three

Black Church: Home Away from Home

"I saw your choir on the Colbert Report with Ambassador Young. I just wanted to say that your performance was very moving and inspirational. Thank you so much for all you do."
–Jesse Keenan
Miami Beach, Florida

"You keep doin' what you're doin', boy, because hell ain't even half-full yet." My mother just loved to say this, as she pushed me into a front-row pew of Greater Refuge Temple, our church on East 133rd Street. And she put me right up front, where our preacher, the beloved pastor, then elder, and later, bishop, Robert C. Lawson, could keep his eye on me, and preach right at me, with his booming voice. I suspect my mother had confided in the pastor that she had to force her hardheaded son, Allen, to come to church, because Bishop Lawson's eyes always seemed to find me in my pew, no matter where I sat in that church.

I was always a little bit scared of this powerful man of God, as I sat there in a shirt and tie with freshly shined shoes, wishing that I could be outside, playing basketball with my friends in the park. But, I was in church every Sunday, unless I was sick.

A tall, husky man with a big, bald head, the handsome Bishop Lawson never needed a microphone. Dynamic, and with a strong voice, he preached inspirational sermons, giving everything he had to motivate his congregation and lift up their spirits. They were hard, hungry times for most everyone living in Harlem back in the late 1940s and '50s.

"Keep going and never give up. Have faith in God and God will take care of you," Bishop Lawson called out, his words and his strength touching us, helping us to carry on. "Those who pray can expect a miracle," he said, pointing right at me. At least, I thought he was pointing at me.

Ours was a small storefront church, which held only about 200 people, but Bishop Lawson was such an inspirational speaker that his Sunday evening service was broadcast on the radio every week. I remember that, right before Bishop passed his hat for donations, he would say, "You know, we can't be on-air, on air," and everyone would smile.

Without a doubt, I am a product of the Black Church. Like many other kids before and since, church kept me well behaved and well fed, at least on Sundays. My mother volunteered as a church usher and a cook, making hearty meals downstairs in the church kitchen, after the morning service. Poor families in the congregation could buy them for just two dollars, or for free, if they had no money coming in.

Church kept me off the streets, out of trouble, and sadly for me, away from my friends. Of the five boys in my family, John, David, Curtis, Bab'Brother and me, I was the second youngest. While the others rose early enough to get out of the apartment before it was time to leave for church at 9AM, I liked to sleep in, and so it fell to me to accompany my mother to Greater Refuge Temple.

My father attended services at a different church in Harlem, and although I sometimes went to church with Dad, my mother usually depended on me to help cut up the vegetables and to take out the garbage, while she cooked and served the food with the other women. Every Sunday, from 10AM to 10PM, we were in church. The big consolation in my mind, at that time, was that I got to eat a really good lunch and dinner, and we took leftovers home, which meant that we had food for at least one or two meals during the week.

In the black community, church was, and often still is, an all-day event. People come in for services, for food, for choir, for community—to just hang out and be together. When I was growing up, black churches were plentiful in Harlem, just like today, and they were the heart and soul of every neighborhood. A refuge from the stress of the week, they were the hub of the community; a place to fill your spirit and your belly, and to give you a sense of belonging. Still, I complained bitterly about being cooped up inside, instead of being out on the basketball court with my friends.

Out of five boys, why was I the one who always had to go with Mom every Sunday? In my heart of hearts, I knew it was because I was the lie-abed who loved to sleep in. I never thought of it as a blessing at the time, but a blessing it turned out to be, and one that became particularly apparent to me many years later. All that time spent in church, listening to Bishop Lawson, trying to avoid his gaze, and wishing I was somewhere else instead of listening to sermons and church choirs—all this gave me the inspiration, the incentive, and the comfort level to begin what would become my life's work: to found, nurture and manage the world's most famous touring gospel choir.

Every service in our church included songs sung by one of the church choirs: the mass choir, the youth choir, the women's choir or the men's choir. Services began with the choir, parading and bopping down through the aisles, to take their place behind the bishop, assistant pastors and the deacons, in the front of the church. Everybody in the congregation joined in those songs that we had heard since we were tiny babies.

Greater Refuge Temple eventually grew to such a large congregation, that it had to move to its own building at the corner of West 124th Street and Adam Clayton Powell Boulevard. The head of the church today is Bishop William Bonner, who was a deacon in the church when I was young. Now, when I go to church, I sit in the back row, sometimes in the balcony, along with the tourists, who flock to the church on the tour buses that can be seen outside so many Harlem churches, on any given Sunday. And still, I am surprised, finding a hand on my shoulder, to turn around and see Pastor Bonner standing there, smiling down on me. It seems that I am always in the front row, when I am in church, no matter where I sit.

It is because of how these church experiences changed and shaped my life and career, that I tell the people I work with in the Choir to get the right attitude about who they are, and what they are doing. Don't complain about where you are right now, because, without a doubt, the experience is helping you get someplace that you need to be later in life. As a kid, all Sunday, every Sunday, I was right where I needed to be—up on East 133rd Street and Fifth Avenue, at the Greater Refuge Temple.

Four

A Divine Birthday

"I love your music, so I decided to invite you to my seventh birthday party. Please RSVP."
—Dictated by Bella and typed by her mom

Not far from the present-day Greater Refuge Temple, on the West Side of Manhattan, on Amsterdam Avenue and 112th Street, at the edge of Ivy-League Columbia University, stands the massive gray medieval-style stone structure of the largest cathedral in North America—the Cathedral Church of Saint John the Divine.

The mother church of the Episcopal Diocese of New York, and the seat of its bishop, the cathedral is a chartered house of prayer that serves the diverse peoples of New York. Like the great cathedrals of Europe, Saint John the Divine's impressive stone structure, and beautiful stained glass windows inspire awe. The church adds old-world beauty to the streets of New York City, which is known mostly for its Midtown skyscrapers, Westside brownstones, apartment buildings, sprawling Central Park and neighborhood stoops.

In my more than six decades of life in New York City, I have passed by and entered into this beautiful cathedral thousands of times: for Black History Month functions, for Harlem Week functions, for Martin Luther King memorial functions. But, perhaps the most memorable function of all, took place on the evening of March 24, 2007, when the world-famous Harlem Gospel Choir had the great privilege of singing at the birthday celebrations for pop-rock superstar, Sir Elton John.

In 2007, Sir Elton turned sixty, and decided to celebrate the milestone with four birthday parties: one in London, one in Sydney, one in New York and one in India. I believe that in the pop star's mind, it was a huge achievement to turn sixty. For so many years, drugs had controlled his life, and many people, including Elton himself, had predicted that he would never reach the venerable sixty mark. However, in March 2007, the singer found himself in Manhattan, performing for no less than the sixtieth time in his long career, at Madison Square Garden. New York loves Sir Elton, and I guess it's only fair to say that Sir Elton loves New York, because he and his longtime partner, David Furnish, selected New York City, and specifically Saint John the Divine, as the venue for one of his extravagant birthday blowouts.

I think that Elton may have been generally aware of the birthday party being planned in his honor, but oblivious to a number of details intended to be a surprise, including the fact that the Harlem Gospel Choir would be part of the evening's entertainment. We were thrilled to hear from David Furnish that, because Elton was a big fan of the Choir, we were a natural choice to perform at Saint John the Divine.

Planning for the celebration was confidential and shrouded in secrecy. Fifteen members of the Choir were booked to sing. Anna and I, worried that word would get out about the top-secret party, told Choir members that on the date in question, they were scheduled to sing at a wedding at Riverside Church.

Gossip and speculation about the party were flying around and the press got wind of it. The paparazzi began calling our office. "Can you tell me in good conscience," one of the press asked Anna over the phone, "that you will not be performing at Sir Elton John's birthday party?" Anna was caught. She didn't want to lie, but she also did not want to blow the surprise, and violate the confidentiality agreement we had been asked to sign. "I can't believe," she shot back to the nosey reporter, "that this is the only reason that you would be interested in the world-famous Harlem Gospel Choir." And with that, she hung up the phone.

After this high-profile booking, Anna was careful, in the future, never to name any venue on our web site, whenever she listed dates for a private function; it was a lesson hard learned. The leak had to have come from a choir member booked to sing at the event. We were both grateful that we had withheld the real venue from the singers, who did not know where it was, until the final studio rehearsal, one day before the dress rehearsal at the cathedral, and two days before the event.

For me, having the Choir sing at this exclusive birthday party was a great milestone in my life. I had originally met Sir Elton, many years before, when I was working on tour with the Commodores. That first meeting took place in February, 1984, during a very hot summer in Sydney, Australia, where Elton, and the Commodores, were both touring separately. We were all staying in the very trendy Sebel Town House, at Double Bay, surrounded by some of the most exclusive shopping in Sydney.

It was at this hotel that Sir Elton embarked on a short-lived marriage, with his good friend and sound engineer at the time, Renata Blauel. Miles from home, like us, the couple graciously invited the Commodores, and members of our group, to attend the wedding reception. It was a fantastic wedding and a beautiful day. Now, twenty-three years later, I was once again participating in a celebration for Elton John, who, after being knighted by the Queen of England herself, no less, was now, Sir Elton John.

When we arrived at the cathedral for the dress rehearsal and sound check, it was obvious that this was going to be a very lavish event. Everything in the church was transformed: All the pews had been removed, and the nave was set with round tables dressed in white tablecloths, and with white chairs, white flowers and fine white china. The guest list was still a secret, even to us, and the cathedral was full of people, moving quickly to set up tables and chairs on a specially laid floor.

While the Choir practiced in a side chapel, and learned the route from the performance area to the dressing room space, I sat at one of the tables to wait, watching the staff prepare the room. To my surprise, someone put a hand on my shoulder and spoke. "Hi, Allen, how are you?" I looked up to see David Furnish, Elton's long-time partner, whom I had first met all those years ago in Sydney, and who had booked us for this celebration. I was so pleased to see him and to discover that he still remembered me. He had been listening to the Choir rehearse. "I am so glad they are here," he said. "I know that Elton is going to love their performance." Not only would the Choir sing "Happy Birthday," but they would also perform two of Elton's songs: "The Circle of Life" and "Border Song."

Returning to the cathedral, the next night, we now found its majestic exterior totally transformed, as well. Anna and I were allowed to park in the private parking area, a great luxury, considering that we were carrying fifteen heavy white robes that we had hired, at David's request, plus our African Kente collars and sashes that we put over the robes to add our trademark color and flavor.

The cathedral's steps were lit up by spotlights and lined with candles. The police were directing traffic as, one by one, limousines delivered attendees from the star-studded guest list. Just a few of the luminaries in attendance that night were Bill Clinton, Paul McCartney, Robin Williams, Bernie Taupin—Sir Elton's longtime writing partner—Donatella Versace, Tony Bennett, Kid Rock, Kiefer Sutherland and Diane Von Furstenberg.

The plan was for the guests to gather in one section of the cathedral for the cocktail hour. Then, as a surprise, the Choir would sing, on an elevated stage in front of the altar, to welcome them, as they moved from cocktails into the dining area. For most of the Choir's first song, however, all the guests remained in the reception area. I think they were really enjoying the pre-dinner drinks and finger food.

So there we all were, fifteen singers in white robes and Kente collars, with Anna and myself, sitting in the choir stalls to the side of the stage, looking down at a room, illuminated by white candles, and furnished with white chairs and tables, decorated with while linens, flowers and china, but with no people, except wait-staff, to see us. At the beginning of the second song, guests finally began to move into the room, and I noticed one elegant lady standing alone, right below the stage, and gazing up at the Choir. It was Diane Von Furstenberg, and she looked to be enjoying the music very much.

As I watched people move, en masse, into the dining area, I saw Elton, dressed in an elaborate tuxedo, enter, and join Diane. Taken by surprise, he stood with his back to his guests and looked up, listening intently. I could see that he was very touched and focused on every word the Choir was singing. I still have the photograph that Anna took of him standing there, looking up at the Choir. Forgive me, Elton, your party planner had told us that no photographs were allowed, but that image of your obvious appreciation was too precious to miss, and I cherish it in my private photo collection.

When the Choir had finished singing "Happy Birthday to You," Sir Elton thanked them. "You guys are terrific," he said. It was high praise, coming from such a talented and successful musician and composer, and it was very generous of him to acknowledge the Choir at all.

Next, an enormous twelve-foot-by-twelve-foot birthday cake was wheeled into the room. Pre-recorded video footage, from absent celebrity well-wishers, was played on huge video screens placed around the room. When the tape finished, Elton gave a beautiful speech, and said what a wonderful evening it had been, and how grateful he felt to be alive in the world, and in a position to do some good, helping others, primarily through his AIDS charity.

As the Choir exited the stage, and walked back to the dressing room, they passed Whoopi Goldberg, who was sneaking a cigarette near one of the exits. We had worked with Whoopi a couple of years earlier for the launch of one of the Norwegian Cruise ships, of which, she is "God Mother." She was always very friendly, so some of the Choir stopped to say hi, and to have their photo taken with her.

It was enthralling and exhilarating that evening in the cathedral to watch so many celebrities enjoy the Choir. And seeing fashion designer, Diane Von Furstenberg there, set me thinking about another time in my life, when I had toured around the world with a troupe of black models.

Back in the 1970s, the fashion industry, except for a few designers, such as Yves Saint Laurent, generally did not accept black models. African-American models did not represent the accepted standards of beauty that designers looked for to sell their clothes. Undeterred, I took a group of black models, both men and women, who could model, sing and dance, on the road. We had the looks, and the talent, but we needed high-fashion clothes to complete our act. Of course, it was difficult to get well-known designers to support us. Diane Von Furstenberg was one of the few who backed our efforts and gave us clothes to take on tour. She was, and still is, a classy gracious lady, and it was a pleasure to run into her again at Sir Elton's birthday party.

At one point, earlier in the evening, as I had stood by a table, waiting as the Choir prepared, I heard a very soft voice whisper in my ear: "Can you please excuse me?" I smelled a beautiful scent and turned around to see a gorgeous woman. It was Elizabeth Hurley, and the fact that she whispered in my ear, just knocked me off my feet. I was smitten and told Anna that I had no plans to wash my ear anytime soon.

Billie Jean King, whom I knew from my work with IMG, helping to promote tennis events, also came over to remind me that she had heard the Choir singing at the Women's Final, at the U.S. Open tennis tournament, in 2001, when the Williams sisters, Venus and Serena, were competing against each other in an historic all-black match. On that special day, Billie Jean had conducted the coin toss, which Serena won, although Venus won the match. "I was really impressed with the Choir tonight," she told me. "I can't tell you what an uplifting performance it was." And, Billie Jean was right, it had been an uplifting performance to help complete a memorable night.

Five

At the Knee of Comedy Great, Pigmeat Markham

"The Choir is so talented and just filled the house with joy! We seldom get to hear nine voices any more skilled than the folks we heard on Friday. I will forever remember the time I spent experiencing their sermon in song."
—Connie, Warrensburg, Missouri

As I already said, my dad, George Bailey, was a born performer, who always craved the entertainer's life, and did take a few turns in Vaudeville. He loved hanging out with entertainers, and he was very proud to be friends with a man, who was, perhaps, Harlem's most famous performer of his day—the great Pigmeat Markham.

Born in Durham, North Carolina, on April 16, 1904, the burlesque comedian, Dewey "Pigmeat" Markham, became famous for his hilarious comedy sketches, including "Heyeah Come da Judge." Pigmeat played the world's funkiest judge. Sitting up high on a judge's bench, sometimes in a black graduation cap and gown to look more impressive, he dealt with a line of comic miscreants. Handing down his "judgments," he would lean over the bench and smack the accused with an inflated bladder-balloon.

"The judge is high as a Georgia pine!" Pigmeat would yell. "Everybody's goin' to jail today! And to show you I don't mean nobody no good, this morning, I'm givin' myself six months! And if I'm gonna do six months, Mr. District Attorney, you can imagine what you're gonna do!" These routines used to bring down the house.

Pigmeat began his career as a tap dancer and then broke into the black Vaudeville circuit. During the late '20s and the '30s, he honed his comedy and skits, playing numerous variety shows. In 1935, he headed north for the Apollo Theater, in New York. Pigmeat's nickname came from an old Vaudeville bit: "Sweet Papa Pigmeat, with the River Jordan at my hips, and all the women is just run up to be baptized!" In Harlem, he was so popular that he sometimes appeared on the Apollo's bill every week for an entire year.

Pigmeat played "Alamo the Cook," during a short stint on the Andrews Sisters' radio show, and he made films that were circulated mostly to black movie houses. In the 1940s, while the *Amos 'n' Andy* show was popular on radio, and the comedy act of Abbott & Costello was adapting burlesque for the movies, Pigmeat was entertaining audiences with his "low" comedy, which he regularly performed in "blackface." This black make-up, paired with big white lips, caused no concerns about racial stereotypes or insensitivity. It was simply viewed as good entertainment for blacks and whites alike.

In the 1950s, Pigmeat Markham made the move to television, appearing numerous times on *The Ed Sullivan Show*. But it was Sammy Davis Jr., who brought him to national attention, when he performed Pigmeat's Heyeah Come da Judge routine on *Rowan & Martin's Laugh-In,* in the late 1960s.

Sammy Davis later took Pigmeat to Vegas with him for a $5,000-per-week gig, just so the older comedian could taste big-time success. Pigmeat also got to perform his signature Judge character for a season on *Rowan & Martin's Laugh-In*. Then, he performed as "Justus O'Peace" on the country show, *Hee-Haw*. All this television work meant that Pigmeat began to cross over, becoming a hit with black and white audiences alike.

"This comic was one of the few greats who walked in the back door so that we young comics of today could walk in the front," comedian George Kirby said in praise of Pigmeat's legacy. "Thank God he has a chance to walk in the front with us. Pigmeat Markham is the greatest."

From the time I was very little, I can remember Uncle Pigmeat, as we called him, being around our family. My dad first met the performer at a barbershop in Harlem called Sugar Ray Robinson, which was the neighborhood hangout. After that, Uncle Pigmeat became a welcome fixture in our life.

When I was a kid, Uncle Pigmeat lived over on Lenox Avenue, not far from us. A tremendous human being, and a family man who loved children, he let me go around with him during the day when I did not have to be in school or church. I loved being with him and realize now that, even at that young age, I was soaking up important lessons from him about what it took to succeed, both as a person and as a professional, in the entertainment business. I still have vivid memories of his massive talent, his warmth and his strong character.

Pigmeat had a beautiful and smooth baritone voice, and his jokes were clean, with no cursing or put-downs; his stuff was very funny and very family oriented. A lot of performers stole from Pigmeat and they were proud to admit it. Most recently, he was even parodied on *The Simpsons*. His humor came from life experience; he had no staff of writers, no big production machine. Everything just flowed from his own observations and experiences. Sammy Davis Jr. always paid homage to him as a pioneer in comedy, saying he learned a lot, just by analyzing Pigmeat's timing, delivery and punch lines.

Uncle Pigmeat instilled in me three important rules for living and working that he often repeated: "Have passion for what you do, respect the people you work for, and be considerate of other people's feelings." It's a very simple recipe for success, if you just have the willingness, humility, and discipline to follow it.

As I grew up, and began a career as an advance man and a tour manager for some of the biggest names in the business, like Frankie Lyman and the Teenagers, in the early days, and later on, for the Commodores, Michael Jackson and Prince, I found myself constantly on the road, just as Uncle Pigmeat had been, and the advice he had instilled in me about how to succeed, stood me in good stead, through all those years.

"First and foremost, Allen," he used to say, "show business is business first, and show second, so take care of business, and everything else will take care of itself." This is a lesson that still serves me well in the challenging world of tour management, where I have to work with promoters and tour operators, as we take the Choir around the world.

From Uncle Pigmeat, I learned to pay close attention, and to make sure that every detail is taken care of today, so that there are no problems tomorrow. It is advice that I passed on to Anna as she took over the management of the Choir. "Your job as manager is to get the money," I constantly remind her. Anyone can take a date and not get paid. In this business, professionals are paid, and because they are paid, they are treated with the respect they need to do their job well.

I couple this with advice that I give to the Choir: every show we do must be performed as if it were our last. If we ever get to the point where we treat our concerts with a lack of respect, and give less than a hundred percent on stage, then that concert may well be our last.

Another of Uncle Pigmeat's favorite quotes that I have made my own is this: "It takes a team to build a dream." Uncle Pigmeat, my dad and I were all great sports fans, and we used to argue about which were the best teams. Back then, Joe DiMaggio was part of the New York Yankees, and Jackie Robinson played for the Brooklyn Dodgers. We always discussed which team we thought had the greatest team spirit.

"The signature of a winning team," Uncle Pigmeat used to proclaim, "is that the individual players all respect each other equally, and work together towards a common goal of winning." I think he was right, and a good example of this is the difference between the U.S. Olympic Basketball teams of 2004 and 2008.

In 2004, America sent an all-star basketball team to the Olympics in Athens, Greece, but the team came back with only a bronze medal, even though everyone had expected them to win gold. The reason? A lot of people thought it was a lack of team spirit and teamwork. Fast forward to the Beijing Olympics in 2008; again America dispatched another illustrious, all-star basketball team, but this time, the team members had great chemistry and worked together perfectly as a team. Each player was willing to sacrifice individual glory as, backed by their coaches, the team worked with a sense of oneness towards a single goal of bringing home the gold, and they succeeded.

Like my dad, Uncle Pigmeat had only a third-grade education, but throughout his career, he applied the simple lessons of respect for self and others, and of personal decency, that still hold true today. "Allen, ditch your ego and just be a nice person," Uncle Pigmeat used to tell me. "The golden rule, of treating others like you want to be treated, will get you much further than trying to be something that you are not. Don't always try to be the most important person in the room." Not a day goes by that I don't think about what the great Pigmeat Markham taught me about life and the business of show business.

Sadly, Uncle Pigmeat died on December 13, 1981. I still miss him and I recently ordered his taped performances from Amazon.com. I really enjoy playing those tapes, when I'm back in my hotel room after a show. They take me back to the days when I had the privilege of hanging out with Uncle Pigmeat. I suggest you do yourself a favor: go online, and buy a DVD or CD of Pigmeat's most popular routines, to witness a comic genius and great American entertainer at work.

Six

Basketball and Music

"I have been here in Vermont for ten years and have NEVER seen Vermonters rocking and dancing and participating in ANYTHING like they did tonight. There was some life bouncing around those walls tonight."
—**Karen, Barre, Vermont**

    I began my career in entertainment on the streets of Harlem when I was about fifteen. I used to play basketball with my friends after school, when we would travel to other schools in Harlem to play pickup games. Not formally organized, these were just games we played with the kids, who were already on the school basketball courts, when we arrived that day.

    One day, I was playing a pickup game at a school called Stith Junior High School, in Washington Heights, in upper Harlem, when I heard a group of kids singing a capella in the hallways of the school. The sound was edgy doo-wop. I loved street music so I stopped playing and went over to listen. Walking into the school, I saw five kids practicing their harmonies, and I recognized the man, who seemed to be in charge of the singers, as Richard Barrett, a very famous singer with a group called the Valentines, that had scored several hit singles.

    I introduced myself and told Richard how much I liked the group. I was really starry-eyed and nervous because he was so famous. He thanked me, and then I went on to say that I had all of the Valentines' 78s (records were 78 vinyl discs at that time), and what an honor it was to meet him.

    The Valentines were very popular in Harlem at the time, and the group had just performed at the famous Apollo Theater; a lot of kids my age idolized them. All six Valentines were tall and good looking with processed hair; they put lye on it to straighten it, just like Nat King Cole, and they wore slick polyester suits and wing-tipped patent leather shoes.

Richard was very kind to me that day; I guess my fascination shone through all my efforts to look cool. He told me that if they ever performed at the Apollo Theater again, he would get a pass for me so that I could attend the concert.

After this meeting, I went up to Stith Jr. High, as often as I could after classes, to hear the group rehearse, and to hang out with Richard. And soon I became friends with other kids he was rehearsing—Joe Negroni, Herman Santiago, Jimmy Merchant, Sherman Garnes and Frankie Lyman. They called their group the Teenagers, and they were rehearsing because Richard had gotten them an audition with his friend, George Goldner at Gee Records, downtown, on Broadway.

Before the audition, Herman was the lead singer, but when George Goldner heard Frankie's voice at the audition, he asked him to sing lead, and Frankie led the group in a song they had written called "Why Do Fools Fall in Love?" Of course the rest is history, and the subject of several books, a movie and more than one lawsuit. But for me, this was a historic connection, and it marked the beginning of my touring career.

At fifteen, I was already six feet tall, and Richard hired me as security for the group, when they had local gigs in Brooklyn, Manhattan, New Jersey and Connecticut. I couldn't travel with them all the time, because I was still in school. The group members went on to attend the New York Professional Children's School on West Sixtieth Street, and I believe that the school sent tutors with them when they toured, because New York City law required it. Another friend of ours also attended Stith, and the New York Professional Children's School—actress, Leslie Uggams.

I became friends with all the guys, but I had the most in common with Sherman. He was one of the truest bass singers I ever heard, and was even taller than I was. We played basketball together on the weekends, when he was in town and not performing. Frankie Lyman had led a much more sophisticated life than I, so I hung on all of the stories he told, and grew to like him very much. I met his parents and all three of his wives! We remained friends until his tragic death, from a heroin overdose, when he was only twenty-five.

My friendship with Richard Barrett gave me an opportunity, one day, to meet a very famous girl group called the Chantels. Richard was an intense, controlling type of guy, and while this meant that he was successful in business, it also meant that he had few friends. He was a strict disciplinarian, who, today, would probably be pegged as a control freak. Since I was young, and keen to learn the ropes, I avoided challenging Richard in any way, so our friendship had a solid footing. He was happy to take the lead to impress me, and I was happy to tag along.

One day, Richard asked me if I would like to attend rehearsal for a new girl group he was developing. The rehearsal was downtown, on Broadway and Fifty-third Street, and when we walked in, I saw five already well-known singers: Arlene Smith (lead), Lois Harris (first tenor), Sonia Goring (second tenor), Jackie Landry (second alto), and Rene Minus (alto/bass)—the Chantels. After the rehearsal, Richard and I went back up town to play pool.

I tagged along to several Chantels rehearsals with Richard, and became good friends with the girls, especially Jackie. She and I had a lot in common; her birthday was also in September, and she used to call me her big brother, even though I was only a year older than she was. Sometimes she called and asked me to go with her to the Apollo to look at other acts. The girls were all very nice and attended St. Anthony of Padua in the Bronx. They studied hard, and rehearsed each song to perfection, and usually went straight home after rehearsal.

Recently, I was thrilled to see Arlene again, after so many years, at one of our gospel brunches at B.B. King's. I was directing the buffet line before the show began, as I like to do when I am in town on a Sunday, when Anna came over to me to tell me that Arlene Smith was in the audience, and would I come by to say hello. It was amazing to see her again, and a little bit sad, because, while she shook my hand politely, she did not seem to know me.

After the show, Arlene approached me at the signing table, and said that during the show, she had realized that it really was me, and that she very much enjoyed the Choir. She took time out to talk to the singers, who were thrilled with her enthusiasm for their performance. Naturally her praise made me feel very proud.

When he saw how much I enjoyed them, Richard began inviting me to other rehearsals with the Chantels, the Teenagers, the Three Degrees, the Valentines, and one time, with Little Anthony and the Imperials, which I remember very well, because the Imperials were rehearsing choreography, and their teacher was a very famous tap dancer called Cholly Atkins.

I paid attention to what Richard taught the group and I liked to try out Cholly's steps. Now, whenever I am on stage with the Choir and come up with a new move, I think back to those days, when I loved going to rehearsals on Broadway, and I realize that my new move is actually an old move that I learned while watching Cholly rehearse the Chantels, the Teenagers, or Little Anthony and the Imperials. Cholly was always a gentleman, and even though he had to work with some very difficult managers, he never let a difficult situation deter him from doing his job; he dealt with everyone graciously.

When Frankie Lyman, Leslie Uggams and the gang went on to the New York Professional Children's School, I went to the High School of Fashion Industries. I was friends with some of the guys who played on their school's basketball team, and they kept telling me what a good school it was, how the teachers respected the students, and took time to help each student on an individual basis, when needed.

This really appealed to me, because the teachers in my schools never seemed to care about their students as individuals. Also appealing to me, was the fact that the school had an excellent basketball team that had made it to the state championships, which were played in Madison Square Garden. An added bonus was a collection of very pretty girls, which included some aspiring fashion models.

To earn extra money, I used my talents in various ways: I had a part-time job, after school, as a messenger boy at a famous company called America's ReWeavers. This was widely credited as being the best re-weaving or garment-repair firm in Manhattan, with many famous clients. It was located on West Fifty-seventh Street, near Carnegie Hall, and my job was to deliver the clothes to the clients after they had been repaired. These clothes were very expensive, and of course, the clients wanted to have small moth holes and cigarette burns invisibly repaired, rather than throw the clothes out, or donate them to thrift stores.

My boss's name was Marty Zimmerman, and he taught me a lot about saving money, and being thrifty. When he was hungry, Marty directed me to go to one of the local delicatessens in the neighborhood, and bring him back a pastrami sandwich on rye with mustard, and a matzoh ball soup.

When I got back to the store, Marty always turned his back to me and removed a piece of pastrami from the sandwich. Then he would hand back the sandwich and say, "Allen, go back, and tell those people that there is not enough meat in this sandwich." So I had to go back and tell the server what Marty had said. Of course, this happened nearly every day, so, after a while, the deli staff stopped yelling at me, and just added more pastrami to the sandwich, with a smile. It was Marty's little game, and we were all happy to play along, especially since the owner of the deli was one of Marty's long-time customers.

My mother and father had always stressed to us that we had to share whatever we had. I felt very fortunate to attend my school, so a few times a year, I would organize a neighborhood talent show at the Harlem Boys Club Auditorium, on 134th Street, between Fifth and Lenox avenues. I handed out flyers that we printed in the school printing shop for my friends to take to their churches.

Kids, aged from twelve to twenty-one, would turn up on show day to perform and compete. We charged no admission, and throughout the evening, I ran a concession stand in the foyer, selling soft drinks, frankfurters, pretzels and candy bars. I used the money from my part-time job with Marty to buy the merchandise, and Marty's lessons in economy and profit taught me how to buy my stock of refreshments for the best price.

The most expensive items were the hot dogs and buns, so I approached the Greek hot dog vendor, Louie, who, for years, had run a stand on the corner of 135th Street and Fifth Avenue, to ask where he bought his supplies. He asked me why I wanted to know, and when I told him my plans for the concession stand, he offered to order the franks and buns for me whenever I needed them, so that I could take advantage of his wholesale prices. He was a very nice man.

My friend Benny Bay helped me run the concession stand, and between us, we made enough money to pay for the merchandise, to pay ourselves, and to make a donation to the Boys Club. I organized several of these talent shows during high school.

In 1956, while I was still in high school, my girlfriend, Sandy, offered me a very unusual way to earn some extra money: The Metropolitan Opera was putting on a performance of Aida, and they needed young, tall African-

Americans to dress as slaves, and carry the litter, in which, the famous dancer, Geoffrey Holder, would ride across the stage. I remember that the litter itself was enormous and grand and weighed a ton, and Geoffrey, who was six-foot-six, was not exactly a lightweight. It took eight of us to carry him just a few feet on that huge stage.

This was a very unique and prestigious way to earn some extra dollars for my mother, and it was big money, in my view. I think we got fifty dollars per person, per night, for as long as that Opera was performed. Plus, I got to go backstage at the Met, and to meet very famous opera stars, as well as the rich and famous society people, who came back to congratulate them.

My love of music and basketball always kept me on a steady path. If we weren't playing in the schoolyard after school, my friends and I would go shoot hoops in the neighborhood park, at Rivington Houses, across the street from Lincoln Projects. One of the men living in Rivington Houses at that time, was Richard Clarke, who established his own executive search firm, in 1957.

Richard always said hi to me as he passed by where we were playing. One day, on his way home from work, he noticed us playing a three-man pickup game, and stopped me. "Something has just come across my desk that I think will be perfect for you," he said. "I think you should take a look at it, so come by my office at 310 Lenox Avenue, tomorrow, if you can." When I did, Richard showed me the application for a job at Elmo Roper and Associates, one of the biggest market research and public opinion polling companies in the country.

The open position was for an office boy/administrative assistant, but Richard told me that there would be an opportunity for me to work my way up in the company. The following day, I went for an interview, at 30 Rockefeller Plaza, and talked to Gus, the office manager. Gus told me about the company, and showed me the different divisions. "Everyone goes by their first name in the office," he explained. "It's a real family atmosphere."

Over the next couple of weeks, I made two or three more trips down to Rockefeller Plaza, and Gus introduced me to Elmo and the other partners. Finally, I received a phone call from Gus. "They want you to come in tomorrow and start work, "he said. "When you get here, go talk to Debbie, who is in charge of payroll, and give her all your information, so she can tell you about the benefits, including the medical and dental insurance."

I loved working for this company. I got to wear my Ivy-League button-down shirts, blue blazers, three-piece suits, collegiate ties and cordovans from Brooks Brothers. And how could I afford such clothes? One of my friends, from the High School of Fashion Industries, had a part-time job as a stock boy at Brooks Brothers, and he used to tell me whenever they had employee sales. He bought what I wanted, and used his employee discount, so I had amassed quite a nice wardrobe by this time.

The work I did for Elmo Roper and Associates was not high profile, but the company was, and still is, one of the most prominent market research firms in the country. Elmo worked closely with Gallup, and with Archibald Crossley, who were also pioneers in the field. The Roper Center, at the University of Connecticut, is the world's largest repository of polling data, with collections spanning the globe, and dating back to the 1930s.

From being around these learned people, I discovered how important it is to understand your customer, and how crucial marketing is to the success of any commercial venture. So, I have a good deal to thank Richard Clarke for. I am so happy that today he has one of the largest, African-American-owned, executive search firms in the country. President Obama reminds me a little of Richard; they have the same positive energy, the same mannerisms, and a larger-than-life personality.

Seven

In the Company of Legends: Miles Davis and Nina Simone

"I'm back home from the concert that the Harlem Gospel Choir gave in Fort-de-France. Oh happy night! Amazing voices and performance! The angels were in Fort-de-France tonight!"
—Tania, Fort-de-France, Martinique

Miles Dewey Davis III: I first met the jazz legend in the late 1950s, when I was still at High School of Fashion Industries. Miles owned a beautiful brownstone building on West Seventy-third Street, between West End Avenue and Riverside Drive. The upper half of the building was beautifully appointed for Miles' personal use; the lower half, he rented out as apartments to struggling artist types. A friend of mine, who had graduated from Fashion Industries, was renting a place there, and a gang of us used to go over and hang out on the street in front of the building, just to socialize and shoot the breeze.

One day, we must have gotten too rowdy, because the front door of the brownstone suddenly flew open, and there stood Miles Davis himself. We all fell silent.

"Hey, you, come here," Miles said, pointing at me. I was the biggest of the bunch, already over six feet, and I guess I stood out. "Are you talking to me?" I asked.

"Yeah, I'm talking to you," Miles said. "Who do you think I am talking to, the tree? Get in here now." He looked annoyed, and I didn't know what to think, as I walked up the steps to the brownstone, and followed the notoriously difficult musician into his house.

Inside, the place was filled with evidence of Miles' massive achievements: certificates, awards, trophies and framed photographs told a story of who he was, the people he knew, and the great things that, still only in his thirties, he had already accomplished.

Miles led me over to the stove, where a pot giving off a delicious aroma, was simmering. He stuck a spoon into the pot, scooped up some mixture, and pushed it at me. "Here, try this," he said," Tell me what you think." It tasted fantastic. "It's delicious," I said. "What is it?"

"It's paella," Miles said, tasting the mixture, himself. "I got the recipe in Spain." And so began my friendship with the legendary musician and complex character named Miles Davis.

At that time, Miles had recently fallen down the steps of his townhouse and injured his leg. At first he wore a cast, and later, he was forced to walk with a cane for a while. I fell into the habit of hanging out at his place, running errands for him, or acting as his guinea pig, whenever he tried new recipes. I was a greedy high school student, and I ate anything that he threw my way. He was a real gourmet cook who believed that good sauces were key to a fine meal. He loved to concoct amazing dishes, mixing the exotic herbs and spices he had found on his travels.

Miles was a musical genius, and like many gifted people so often can be, he was very high strung. He had a well-publicized drug habit, and he kept himself under constant stress, continually feuding with people or getting worked up about something. He trusted few, so I was gratified that he invited me, into his life, to join only a handful of people he kept close at the time.

I think that my lighthearted nature, and the fact that I was always smiling, were a source of both pleasure and irritation for Miles. On the one hand, I was easy on the nerves, and helped to distract him from his stresses, strains and ongoing feuds, but on the other hand, my constant optimism annoyed him. "What are you smiling for?" he would growl at me. "I'm smiling because I am alive," I answered one time. "It's better to be above ground than below ground," I said. Miles gave me a look with those black eyes that could burn right through you, and shook his head.

Miles had two kids, a son and a daughter. Miles Jr. was a bit of a rebel and always getting into scrapes; nothing bad, just liked to do things his own way. His daughter, Shirl, lived in St. Louis, where Miles had family, but she flew in to help her dad after his leg injury. I had a little car at the time, and I took Shirl around town, running all Miles' errands. Soon, Shirl and I began to date a little, or to see each other, as it was called back then. Shirl was a wonderful girl, attractive, good natured and intelligent.

Miles had two sides: he could be very warm, loving and generous, but he was also apt to be bitter and critical. At that time, he was seeing a lady called Frances who lived out in California. She was traffic-stopping beautiful and looked like a young Dorothy Dandridge. She used to fly back and forth from California to New York to see Miles, until eventually they got married, and then she moved into the brownstone. After that, she was trapped with him, and his frequent bad moods.

Frances was incredibly sweet natured and had enough patience to put up with all of Miles' nonsense. When Miles became obnoxious, Frances wisely chose not to fight back. Instead, she would tiptoe away to the sanctuary of an upstairs room, to read the books she loved, or to write in her journal, until Miles had calmed down. I didn't like the way that Miles picked on Frances, so, if he did this while I was visiting, I did my best to distract him. A few years ago, I was on tour with the Choir, in California, when I ran into Frances at the Dome. The beautiful woman I once knew, has grown into a sweet old lady who still radiates warmth and gentleness.

As I said, Miles trusted very few. At that time, the small group surrounding him, included only Shirl; Frances; Miles' longtime lawyer; Roger, a young tenant from one of the downstairs apartments; and myself. Roger was a struggling actor, and Miles let him live rent-free, in exchange for his doing errands and odd jobs. Roger appreciated the apartment, but Miles made him work for it. He would ring Roger up late at night, or in the early hours of the morning, to complain that something in his house wasn't working, and to get up here, now, and fix it.

Later on, when I lived on East Seventy-seventh Street, directly across town from Miles' house on the West Side, he would call me up to ask me to listen to some piece or other that he had composed. He would play it so loud that I had to hold the phone away from my ear. His arrangements were so sophisticated, as he continually tried to reinvent himself, transcending traditional jazz, and taking the music to another place that was uniquely his own.

Later on, I became good friends with basketball great, Kareem Abdul-Jabbar, who was an absolute jazz nut. I would take him to visit Miles, and all they talked about was jazz, jazz, jazz—all day long. Miles was a big boxing fan, and he used to kid me that he could knock out the giant, Kareem, with no problem. "I'll just punch him in his knees and take him down," Miles joked.

Miles and I spent a lot of time watching or talking about boxing. Miles loved the sport and tried to school me in its finer points. One retired boxer he greatly admired was James Braddock, also known as "Cinderella Man," who was, according to Miles, one of the few fighters who could lead with his right to knock an opponent down; an uncommon talent, apparently. Miles liked Sugar Ray Robinson for the same reason. Miles and I used to shadow box, with him showing me all the moves, how to throw a right and a left and an uppercut.

Because of the time I spent with Miles, I was privileged to meet some of the greats in African-American culture and entertainment. Miles was jazz royalty, and he was working with other formidable musicians at that time, like Herbie Hancock and John Coltrane, who would stop by to see him, to play, or to just hang out. And not just musicians came by, there were writers, producers and actors—a steady stream of talent coming in and out.

Just farther along the road from Miles' place, on West End Avenue, lived the handsome and talented entertainer, Harry Belafonte, and his exquisite wife, Julie, one of the most beautiful, poised and gracious women I have ever met. Frances and Julie were friends, so I was invited to the Belafonte residence for a social gathering. What a place! At least twelve rooms and something I couldn't get over—an elevator that opened directly into their apartment. I had never seen such a thing.

Later, Miles told me that when Harry had applied to the coop board, which governed who could and could not take up residence in the building, the board had turned him down. Harry got mad and he also got even: he shelled out millions to buy the entire building, so that he could, if he wished, enjoy the privilege of asking members of the coop board to leave.

A few years ago, the Choir performed in an event with Harry Belafonte, at Carnegie Hall. He looked wonderful, and as we shook hands, I reminded him of who I was, and asked him to give my warm wishes to Julie; they had been married at least sixty years by then, I believe.

Miles, too, was wealthy. One time, I remember, he received a call from an office that distributed royalty checks, telling him to come and claim uncollected monies. "A check for Bob Dylan in the amount of fifty thousand dollars has also been sitting in my desk for a very long time," the caller confided to Miles. "You can add his check to mine," Miles joked, "and I'll come by and pick them both up."

Miles had spent, I don't know how many hundreds of thousands of dollars, treating himself to a red Ferrari Testarossa; all that money and it was only a two-seater! I didn't get it. Although this high-speed, high-performance automobile looked like a beautiful space-age machine, when I tried to fit my long frame into it, my knees were pushed up against my chest. Miles drove that sports car like he was a race driver. Wearing special gloves and goggle-type glasses, he would take off at high speed and go screeching around the neighborhood. He loved that car, and it sure was beautiful, but I didn't like riding in it; too tight.

You have to remember that in the 1950s and 1960s, Manhattan, and Harlem in particular, was a hot bed of social, political, cultural and entertainment revolution. The Civil Rights Movement was gathering steam, fueled by leaders from Harlem, and performers flocked to the Apollo Theater—a mecca for black entertainers. It was an amazing time to be young and alive, and to forge life-altering relationships with people who were literally changing the world; people like Miles, who were well on their way to becoming, if they were not already, living legends. Not too long after I met Miles Davis, I was blessed to encounter another living legend—Ms. Nina Simone, the high priestess of soul.

By the time I met Nina, I had graduated from high school. Upstairs, in the building where I lived, was a young sister called Pam, who worked as an au pair for a woman, whose name she would not reveal, and whom she would not discuss, except to claim that she was very, very, very famous. "Famous people are always coming by to see her," Pam confided, but she would not say just who these mystery VIPs were.

As Pam and I became firm friends, we palled around more and more, until one day she asked me for an unexpected favor: "My employer has to attend a fundraiser uptown in Harlem at the Apollo," Pam said, "and she needs an escort who knows the neighborhood. You interested?"

"You're gonna have to tell me who it is first," I said.

"It's Nina Simone," Pam said, and I was blown away. Nina was only seven years older than I was, but she was a world away in sophistication. "Do I have to wear a tuxedo?" I asked, "because I don't have one." Pam made a few calls to get the details about the event: what I should wear, and when I should pick up Nina. "Just come smart but casual, and escort Ms. Simone to the Apollo for 7PM," came my instructions.

At the time, I was driving around town in a small used Pontiac, but I cleaned it, and showed up for my "date" with Nina Simone. She looked stunning and very regal in a beautiful cape-coat with a hood. I chauffeured this beauty uptown, and as I escorted her inside the theater, I stood back, trying to keep out of the way, as people thronged around, eager to greet her. Backstage, the singer ran through a quick sound check, and then we were shown to our seats, in the house.

The gala was a star-studded fundraiser for Dr. King and his Civil Rights projects, and Nina was scheduled to go on at 10PM to give the last performance of the evening. But, as is typical, the show ran late, and Nina sat fidgeting as she waited to go on. Finally, it was her turn to take the stage, and she wowed the crowd with two songs: "Mississippi Goddamn," a song that she recorded, and from which she donated the profits to the Civil Rights cause; and "Black Is the Color of My Loved One's Hair," a trademark song of hers that brought down the house that night, driving the crowd of VIPs and press onto their feet for a long, uproarious standing ovation.

When she finally left the stage, Nina wanted to go straight home, and skip the after-party. While she was not as high-strung as Miles, Nina could nevertheless be intense, and not one for cocktail crowd get-togethers, small talk and social chitchat.

Back at her apartment, on the West Side, I tried not to listen in as Nina made calls to Miriam Mekeba, the great (and recently deceased) South African singer. Nina also got on the phone to talk to Odetta, another South African performer. She laughed and kidded and talked about how the evening had gone. Miriam called Nina by the nickname that all her friends used—Sassy. Not shy about expressing her opinions, Nina could run her mouth, and I guess that's how she earned the name, Sassy.

After that night, I started seeing more of Nina, and although she was still only in her twenties, I learned that she was already very disillusioned with America. She later moved to France and spent most of her of time in Europe, because she felt that she and her children would be treated better there, and she was right. She went on to become a megastar in France, where she passed away at her home in 2003, at age seventy.

Nina could be bitter about America and the struggle for rights that we faced as African-Americans. She used to express frustration with what she thought was my complacency about Civil Rights issues. She was incorrect, I was not complacent, I wanted the same things that she and all my brothers and sisters did—justice and equality, dignity and respect. I simply had my own methods for going about achieving this: prayer and meditation, quiet and steadfast determination and action. I didn't see the point of running around yelling and screaming.

I recently went to dig up my old vinyl Nina Simone recordings from storage, but I found them ruined, so I went out and bought them as CDs. Her voice was astonishing, and I remember her as a great influence on young black women. Nina thought that respect should be earned and not given, and that a woman ought to carry herself with such dignity that there was no doubt about how she wanted to be treated. Nina believed that a black woman was the queen of the universe, and that's how she held herself—like a queen.

Eight

The Motown Years

"What a marvelous show! Your songs and lyrics touched my heart and my soul. Although my father died only a few weeks ago, your message of love made me feel better."
—Rüdiger, Dortmund, Germany

At the same time that I was working for Elmo Roper and Associates, I continued to hang out, after work, with Richard Barrett and his friends. Sometimes my cousin, Jimmy Caster, who was, and still is, a very famous singer and songwriter, would join us. Richard had a big Lincoln Continental, so we would pile in, and ride all the way out to Coney Island. After we had eaten as many hot dogs as we could stuff down ourselves, Richard would dare us to see how long we could stay on the Cyclone.

The Cyclone is one of the most famous roller-coaster rides at Coney Island; the average ride lasts about two to three minutes, and then it stops to let new riders on. We paid extra to ride longer, but I usually only lasted about five minutes, because, while the upward climb was okay, the drop, once the car had reached the top of the track and then plummeted, was hard to take. Jimmy could last for a few more minutes. Richard, however, loved the entire ride and could outlast everyone.

Richard was older than the rest of us and was an ex-military man. We used to tease him: "Hey, old man, you're too old to be doing this, old man," we kidded. And of course, this would wind up his ego, and egg him on to challenge us. "We'll see about that, you young whippersnappers," he shot back as he paid for more time on the Cyclone. He must have had a strong stomach, because he never got tired of the ride, and he never got sick, no matter how many hot dogs he ate.

Sometimes, instead of driving around in the Lincoln Continental, we played pool in Harlem's pool halls. My favorite was in Washington Heights, where all the top billiard players gathered on Monday, Wednesday and Friday nights to hustle each other. These guys fascinated me; they were so talented and skilled. One guy was so good that his nickname was Eight Ball, and he used only one hand to play. His skill and rap enthralled me. "Anybody want to take me on?" he would ask the crowd. "I'll play you with one hand behind my back." That was the bait.

"How much are you betting?" he would ask as punters put their money on the table; then there were side bets on who would win. Since no one, who knew him, would bet against him, Eight Ball had to move from pool hall to pool hall to earn his living. I noticed that occasionally he would let the other person win, just to entice more people to bet against him, and to increase the pot. The betting was too rich for my blood at that time—fifty to a hundred dollars per game—so I never got to play against these guys. But Jimmy and Richard both tried their skills against Eight Ball, and they both lost.

I remember another pool hustler called Muscle Head who was on the local circuit. His specialty was putting the cue behind him to shoot from around his back. Just like Eight Ball, he was unbeatable, too. Those guys, Muscle Head and Eight Ball, did not play against each other out of mutual respect. Each one controlled a table in the pool hall, and the patrons would go from table to table, trying to beat them. Both guys were impeccably dressed with alligator shoes and diamond pinky rings. Hustling pool was how they made their living, and each man could take home up to $200 per night, tax free. That was a lot of money back then.

During this time, I also organized "Get-Togethers" to earn extra money. I was still playing basketball for the Harlem Boys Club "Juniors," and for the Beaux Arts, the team that took me to Stith High School. Beaux Arts got its name from one of the players called Richard Wilks, who was nicknamed "Foots," because he had big feet.

By now, we had quit trekking to other high schools looking for a game; that ended when we left school. Now we played in local community centers. We had to raise money to buy uniforms for the team, and so we would pile into someone's apartment on a Friday or Saturday night, where we could sell "fish fry" dinners, which included very greasy fish that our girlfriends used to fry in lard.

The girls supported us by coming to our games and wearing our colors—orange, black and green. To raise money, we charged admission to these "Get-Togethers"—forty-five cents' admission, with a ticket, and fifty-five cents' admission, without a ticket. The fish dinners were a dollar fifty. We also sold soft drinks—lemonade and Kool-Aid.

These socials also helped bring the community together. We invited teams from the Bronx, and in turn, they invited us to their get-togethers. We were all in the same boat—none of us had any money, and so after leaving high school, I did not go to college immediately. I stayed home, and helped my mother, working for Elmo Roper during the day, and managing a hectic social life at night.

After I left high school, I was accepted to Central State Ohio and Saint Augustine's College (St. Augs) in North Carolina. Both had offered me a basketball scholarship, but during the two years I had been working, I had injured my knee playing social football in McCoombs Dam Park near Yankee Stadium. I tore a ligament in my left knee, and while I could still play basketball, I could not sustain the intensity of play needed for a college scholarship. So, because of a freak accident, I lost my college scholarship and had to apply for a student loan. To help out, when I finally left the firm to go to college, Elmo Roper and the staff bought me luggage, and gave me money for school supplies.

I had just turned twenty, when I began my freshman year at Central Ohio State, a school I chose because I already had so many friends among the student body there. I felt comfortable knowing that I had a built-in social circle waiting for me. Still, at the end of the bus ride from Harlem to Wilberforce, Ohio, when I looked out of the window of the bus and saw cattle, sheep and rolling green fields, it did take me back a bit. This was really a change of scenery for me, and I knew that my life was going to be quite different from the one I had lived in New York.

My roommate was a guy named Butch Whittaker, whose family ran the largest funeral parlor in Columbus, Ohio. On that first day, when I arrived in the room we would share, Butch was already in residence, and busy marking his territory by putting up little signs that read: "We will be the last to let you down" and "Our customers never complain." As I sat on my bed, taking in the signs, Butch told me to stand up. When I did, he took a tape measure out of his pocket. "My family is running a big sale on caskets and burial plots," he said. "I am going to give you a deal on one of each."

"What happens if I get lost at sea after I buy my casket?" I asked. "Are you going to give me a refund?" Butch burst out laughing and we became instant friends. Butch was a strange guy who wore horrific aftershave that I am almost certain was embalming fluid; it certainly smelled like embalming fluid. I used to joke with him that I slept on the top bunk with one eye open, just in case he ever felt the need to drum up business for the family.

Butch sometimes drove me to his family home in Columbus on the weekends; they lived above the funeral parlor. When he brought someone home for the first time, he would call ahead to tell the family that he was bringing a guest. I later discovered that this was part of a set-up.

When we arrived at his residence, Butch took me on a tour of the funeral parlor, and showed me bodies in various stages of being embalmed, and prepared for burial. As we walked past the caskets, a hand reached out from one and grabbed my arm. In shock, I yelled, and must have jumped a mile. Butch laughed and laughed, doubling over with glee.

One of the funeral parlor employees had climbed into the casket before I arrived, and then lain there, waiting to grab me as I walked by. Butch's calling ahead, to announce that he was bringing home a guest, was the cue to play the practical joke on the latest unsuspecting visitor. Throughout the year, Butch would play jokes like this one on all of us.

As freshmen, we were given the opportunity to serve on various student committees, and I opted to work with the committee responsible for bringing entertainment to the campus. Because of my knowledge and background, they asked me to chair the committee, and to help book acts.

The first artist I ever booked for the college was huge—the Queen of Soul herself, Aretha Franklin. It came about because I knew Aretha's manager, Ruth Bowen, who later became a very good friend of mine. Ruthie, as her friends called her, was the first black female booking agent in America. I had met her one night, some years back, when I was still in High School. I was at the Apollo with my girlfriend, Sandy Bussant, where we had gone to see Uncle Pigmeat, and Dinah Washington, who was sharing the bill with him.

Of course, we went backstage to congratulate Pigmeat, and it was there that I saw Ruthie, who, as Dinah's manager, was busy collecting the performance fee for the singer. I introduced myself to Ruthie because I was so thrilled to see her there. I had seen pictures of her in the newspaper, and knew that she represented several very famous black artists, including Sammy Davis Jr. and the Isley Brothers.

Now in college, and keen to make an impact by booking Aretha, I called Ruthie and asked her when the singer would be available. As it turned out, Aretha was already on tour and Ruthie told me that, if I waited, she could fit my date into Aretha's tour schedule. Plus, I could get a good price, since the date fell on a weeknight rather than a weekend.

I was very excited on the day of the show, because Aretha had never performed at our university before, and the gymnasium, which we had converted into a concert hall for the event, was expected to be full. As it turned out, the singer and her band were late for sound check, because her bus driver got lost. This was before the age of cell phones, so there was no way for him to call the school to get directions. The student committee was very anxious, because we only had a set time for sound check, and the sound in gymnasiums is always problematic.

Aretha finally arrived and told us not to worry; everything was going to be fine. She and her band went straight to the stage to complete a mini sound check. Naturally the concert was wonderful, and everyone was very happy, which put a feather in my cap with the committee.

Later on, Ruthie and I constantly talked about other artists she managed who were headed to Ohio on tour. We got very lucky because Motown had a caravan of artists coming through Ohio that winter. You would not believe the names on that tour: Diana Ross and the Supremes; the Temptations; the Four Tops; Stevie Wonder; Smokey Robinson and the Miracles; Martha Reeves and the Vandellas; the Contours; and several other acts. Ruthie agreed to book the caravan for the school, since I had proved to her that I could produce a successful concert at our venue. Again, the show was a huge success.

Over the years, Ruthie and I always stayed in touch. In 1997, Anna and I visited her in Florida. We went down there for a trade conference run by *Performance Magazine*, at which, Ruthie was one of the celebrity speakers.

Retired by then, Ruthie spent much of her time in Miami, where she had a winter home. She took us to a wonderful local restaurant called The Stoned Crab.

In April 2009, I had to say goodbye to Ruthie after she finally lost her battle with brain cancer, at the age of eighty-four. Her funeral was held at Canaan Baptist Church in Harlem, and the building was filled with her friends and colleagues, truly a who's who of the entertainment world. Aretha sang, Cissy Houston sang, and Dionne Warwick spoke about her relationship with Ruthie over the years. Many Harlem dignitaries were there, including Congressman Charles Rangel, and one of Ruthie's oldest friends, Mayor David Dinkins. I was caught by surprise, when her husband, Ace (Billy Bryant), called me over and asked me to be in procession, as the casket was carried in and out of the church. I was in good company with Duke (of the Four Tops), Reverend Al Sharpton, Lloyd Price, and Duke Ellington's niece, Mercer Ellington. I will miss Ruthie who really was my first contact with Motown.

Nine

Dr. King and the March on Washington

"I was at your concert in the Czech Republic in Liberec. It was wonderful. Jesus was there with you. Thank you for your work in our nation."
—**Petra, Czech Republic**

Probably the most dramatic event that marked my coming of age in Harlem, was the historic March on Washington for Jobs and Freedom, which took place on August 28, 1963, when I was twenty-three years old. It was on this day that Dr. Martin Luther King Jr. delivered his memorable "I Have a Dream" speech, in front of the memorial of the great emancipator, Abraham Lincoln, and before a crowd reported to be as many as 300,000 strong.

The March on Washington represents an iconic happening in American history, and for me personally, it was one of the most influential and galvanizing events of my life. On that summer's day, I traveled with a group that included such high-profile coordinators of the march as Percy Sutton and Basil Paterson.

Percy Sutton was one of America's best-known lawyers at the time, and noted for such controversial clients as Malcolm X. Since then, Percy has been an important and long-time politician and activist in Harlem, who has done massive amounts for the community, including leading the revitalization of the Apollo Theater. Basil Paterson is the father of New York State's first black governor, David Paterson, who recently stepped into this top job, when Governor Eliot Spitzer resigned because of a sex scandal. Basil was deputy mayor of New York City in 1963, and went on to have a career as a New York state senator, and as a secretary of state. Needless to say, I was very excited to be at the center of the action and among such influential players.

The day before the march, our group headed out in a van with Percy Sutton and the other coordinators. It was very hectic, because we had to make sure that all the buses carrying people to the march from Harlem, left on time. Various churches were frantically trying to coordinate their members so it was pretty rough for everyone involved. I was impressed with the fact that nobody got hurt and everyone got to the march safely.

When they introduced Dr. King to the crowd, I may have been three or four rows back. It was a warm day, so I decided to sit in the shade to watch the speech. All of us in that huge gathering, black and white, celebrities and regular folks, alike, were spellbound by Dr. King's immortal and inspired words.

After the speech, as I mingled in the crowd, I met many fascinating people, including one great New Yorker, a gentleman, diplomat and judge named Mr. Arthur Goldberg, who had argued famously against the death penalty. In 1962, President John F. Kennedy had appointed him to be an Associate Justice of the Supreme Court, a post he later resigned to become President Lyndon Johnson's appointee, as U.S. ambassador to the United Nations. Arthur Goldberg was very prominent and influential, and it was later reported that Sirhan Sirhan, who assassinated Robert Kennedy in 1968, had included Arthur on his assassination list.

Some years later, in 1970, I helped Arthur campaign when he went up against Nelson Rockefeller for the post of governor of New York, at the same time that Basil Paterson ran for lieutenant governor of New York. Arthur lost, largely because he was woefully outspent by Nelson Rockefeller, who used his personal fortune for marketing, which included buying all the available billboards in New York!

When I told Arthur that my strengths were in coordinating, he introduced me to a guy named Jerry Bruno, who worked for him, and more notably, for the Kennedys, as an advance man. His job it was to go ahead of a candidate to an event, to get the crowd warmed up, and to make sure that everything was running smoothly. Bruno took me under his wing and taught me all the ins and outs of being a good advance man. He was the best in the breed, so I got to study at the knee of a real master. For a good read, and a behind-the-scenes look at the Kennedy campaign mystique, check out Jerry's book, *The Advance Man*, which he wrote with Jeff Greenfield's help.

Looking back, I think that Arthur was too nice to win the governorship. From my observations of Harlem politicians, he didn't seem to possess the same toughness and fire. He shied away from dirty politics, refusing to speak ill of anyone. The Rockefeller camp, by contrast, threw everything they could at Goldberg and spared no insults or innuendos. They were always in attack mode. Even so, Arthur always pushed ahead with his plan, supported by his lovely wife, Barbara. I think that if Arthur had won his bid for governor, I might have earned a post in his office, and ventured further into politics and government.

Through working with Arthur, I met a wonderful group of people who were prominent in New York at that time, including Eugene Nickerson, who became a New York judge; Rich Zitrin, a very prominent entertainment attorney; and Arthur Kaminiski, and his wife, Andy. Arthur was an attorney, representing a number of high-profile hockey players, who played for teams like the Rangers and the Islanders. He lived out on Roslyn, Long Island, a beautiful section of Nassau County, New York. It was such a relief for me to go out there, away from the grime of the city, to relax and daydream. "One of these days," I used to tell myself, "I will have one of these places for myself." I was always the city kid dreaming about having a weekend escape from Manhattan.

After Arthur lost his bid for the governorship, I stayed in touch with him, and with the group of supporters who had tried to get him elected governor. One day, in the early 1980s, I saw Arthur again. I was on Thirty-fourth Street in front of Macy's, collecting petitions to help establish Dr. Martin Luther King's birthday as a national holiday. Arthur seemed genuinely happy to see me. "Be sure and call me if you need anything," he said. I took him at his word, asking his office to help me coordinate signatures and petitions. Our campaign efforts were nationwide, and I recall that we had a very tough time in Arizona, which, according to feedback from our volunteers there, was pretty much opposed to the national holiday. I remember Arthur Goldberg fondly, and thank him and all those friends in Nassau County, Long Island, who did so much to help us in Harlem.

One of my proudest moments ever, came when I received a special commendation from Coretta Scott King, Dr. King's widow, and from Julie Belafonte, wife of the iconic singer, Harry Belafonte. These were both very strong, beautiful women, whom I deeply admired, because each one had a very powerful husband, but still managed to maintain her own identity.

The commendation was for my work on the committee that helped to make sure that the Martin Luther King Holiday Bill passed. Both Coretta and Julie did everything they could to support the various organizations campaigning for the holiday. They never hesitated to offer advice or send out a representative to help us. I had my photo taken with each of them, and I still cherish the memory of those photo sessions.

Ten

A Very Big Man: Kareem Abdul-Jabbar

"I have been a fan of southern gospel music for as long as I can remember, and your performance was the pinnacle, the doctorate of gospel music!"
—**Gary, Canada**

In my early twenties, inspired by Dr. King, by the Civil Rights Movement, and by the growing social activism around me, I worked as a community organizer in Harlem and met someone, who would go on to become a true Harlem legend, and a man I am proud to call a good friend: the great athlete and intellect, whom the world now knows as Kareem Abdul-Jabbar.

Kareem was born Ferdinand Lewis Alcindor Jr., in Harlem Hospital, on April 16, 1947. Kareem's mother always called him Lewis, but his friends called him Lew or El Cid, after the Charlton Heston character in the 1961 movie, *El Cid*. Lew earned the name El Cid, because we compared what he did on the basketball court, at that time, to what the El Cid character did on the battlefield: defeat the enemy. After he converted to the Nation of Islam, Kareem cast off his old name, Lew, and the ties to slavery that he believed it represented, and he took the name Kareem Abdul-Jabbar.

Kareem grew up in the Dykeman Street Projects at 175th Street and Dykeman. We spent quite a bit of time together in Harlem during our younger days, and it was there that we both began our careers as community activists. When he was seventeen, Kareem got a job with an antipoverty program called HARYOU-ACT. I was seven years older than Kareem, and working with Job Corps, a job-training program for youths. We used to run into each other at meetings now and then. Kareem also had a part-time job, working in a custom shirt shop, on Madison Avenue at Fifty-second Street. I would go in for a visit, and always ask him to show me shirts from the top shelf, just to see him stretch his big body and give him a workout.

We had a lot of fun, and spent a good bit of time hanging out at Snookie's Sugar Bowl on 137th Street and Seventh Avenue, where kids congregated, and dressed collegiate in button-downs, White Buck blazers and cardigan sweaters. I remember Kareem had some fancy threads, and wore better-looking stuff than the rest of us, because he shopped at the tall men's shop.

Kareem always preferred to hang out with the older guys, because I don't think he had much in common with kids his own age. I suspect that his mother was not thrilled about his running with an older crowd, but he had no problem; he was well accepted. Even then, Kareem was into jazz and history and intellectual pursuits. He was mature, and always in his books, and so he related better to older kids than to those his own age.

One of my most vivid memories of Kareem is of the evening that we were out driving in an old station wagon that belonged to HARYOU-ACT. We were headed upstate to attend a conference on running community activist organizations. It was late at night, as I took my turn at the wheel to drive up the New York State Thruway, and then along a dark country road, when a deer suddenly leapt out in front of me.

Unable to stop the car fast enough, I ploughed right into the poor animal. I was shaking as I got out of the car, yelling to Kareem, who was in the back seat of the station wagon, and had managed to sleep through the collision. "Kareem, get up, I just hit a deer!" I cried. Kareem woke up and started cracking up. He used to laugh at pretty much everything I did back then.

I guess somebody alerted the state troopers, because before long, an officer arrived on the scene, and informed us that we would have to wait until morning for our car to be towed to a garage in the nearest town. Kareem was already pretty famous by then, and somehow, word got around that we were staying in a nearby motel. The next morning, a gang of locals woke us up to tell us that our car was being repaired, and to invite us to feast on the deer I'd knocked down. Always good-natured, Kareem ate the deer meat, but I couldn't bring myself to consume the poor animal that I had accidentally killed. During this period, we were full of optimism and a sense of adventure, and these were the kinds of scrapes we got into.

Back in Harlem, on 158th Street, a bunch of us played basketball at a playground that we called the Battle Ground; it was a real tough place. The guys who hung out there were mostly hoodlums and aggressive basketball players, who had to earn respect by pushing, shoving and name-calling; whatever it took to win. Battle Ground might have looked like a playground, but there was anything but play going on during those games. Kareem got some pretty tough training there; it gave him a great foundation for his future life on the basketball courts of UCLA and the NBA.

During his first year in college at UCLA, I flew out to Los Angeles to help Kareem pick up a car, and drive it cross-country back to New York. There was just one small problem: the car was a stick shift, which I had no idea how to drive. So when it came my turn at the wheel, every time I had to change gears, I pressed the clutch, and Kareem shifted the gear. We did this for three thousand miles! I suspect Kareem didn't tell me the car was a stick shift, because, he knew that, had I known, there was a very good chance I might not have agreed to the road trip.

During our long drive, we stopped in several parts of the country. Now that Kareem was famous, and almost universally recognized, we were careful to avoid places where we thought he would be mobbed by autograph seekers. We trekked through the desert, where there was nothing but buzzards, and later, we covered the Texas panhandle, struggling to find a place where we could eat in peace and quiet, without intrusions from fans.

Kareem had already broken all the basketball records, and the National Collegiate Athletic Association (NCAA) officials thought that he was too dominant a player, who could dunk the ball at will, and was virtually unstoppable. So, the powers that be changed the rules to forbid dunking in college games. This was called the Alcindor Rule. But, despite the Alcindor Rule, UCLA still dominated college basketball, and people couldn't get enough of Kareem whose face was all over the magazines.

My father knew Kareem's dad, Lew Alcindor Sr., who was a Juilliard graduate, and an amazing saxophone player. My father used to see Lew Sr., when he performed at the senior citizen centers in the projects. I always wondered why Kareem never played an instrument considering how much he loved music.

During the summer, we tried to go to all the concerts in town, because Kareem was constantly thinking and growing, a voracious learner who inquired about everything around him. He was always talking about history and African-American culture, and he went on to write an excellent book about the amazing cultural influences that came out of Harlem and the Harlem Renaissance. It is called *On the Shoulders of Giants*.

When Kareem graduated, I was well into my career, touring with rock groups. I was busy traveling the country, but I made sure to watch television to keep up with his progress. I just knew that he would be drafted into the NBA. Sure enough, he was picked up by Milwaukee in the first round, and I called to congratulate him. "From Harlem to Milwaukee," I kidded him, and he joked that there was nothing but beer out there. "You had better stay inside then," I said, "because you don't drink."

Later on, Kareem was traded to the LA Lakers, where he played with the great Magic Johnson. He always called or stopped by to see me after the game, if he played Madison Square Garden, and he would introduce me to his team mates. "This is my main man, Allen," he would say. Kareem never forgot his friends or where he came from. He has a great memory, so I call him up when I can't remember things, because he does a great job of recalling all those details that elude me.

Eleven

Changing the World

"God bless you in your ministry to others, to the nations, and to the children. I was amazed how willingly the people in Moscow, who need God, were ready to worship him with you."
—Elena, Moscow

Throughout the 1960s, young people were inspired to action by our great, and in some cases, fallen black leaders, by the Kennedy brothers, and by the Civil Rights Movement. Kareem and I became passionately involved in social and civil rights programs. As I have said, we both worked in Harlem, as activists, to improve conditions for poor black kids in our community, much in the same way that a young Barack Obama would later work to help communities on the South Side of Chicago.

Kareem and I were involved in the antipoverty group, HARYOU, which was short for Harlem Youth Opportunities Unlimited, and founded by Dr. Kenneth Clark in 1962, and directed by Cyril DeGrasse Tyson. The group worked to increase opportunities in education and employment for young blacks in Harlem. It also was designed to teach local community organizations, in Harlem, how to work with government agencies to meet their demands, in order to obtain government grants.

In 1964, the Johnson administration provided $110 million to back educational changes, recommended by HARYOU. These plans included recruiting educational experts to reorganize Harlem schools, providing preschool programs, after-school remedial education, and employment programs for dropouts. HARYOU merged with Associated Community Teams (ACT) under the encouragement of Congressman Adam Clayton Powell, Jr. The combined entity took the name HARYOU-ACT.

Since there was now money available from the federal government for these kinds of programs in Harlem, I, along with several community activists applied for, and received, a grant to recruit young men and women to join the Job Corps, one of the programs under the HARYOU-ACT banner

I was executive director for the Central Harlem Job Corps from 1964 to 1966, and our office was in the YMCA at 135th Street and Adam Clayton Powell Boulevard. (The YMCA is still there today, but our office is long gone.) My job was to recruit sixteen to twenty-one-year-old young men and women, who were willing to learn the basic skills that they needed to find employment, such as refrigeration repair, motor mechanics, typewriter repair, electrical repair, food services, general office management and what have you.

The recruits went to training facilities, scattered throughout America, where they would also study to pass their GEDs. It was a very successful program started by the Kennedy and Shriver family. I was twenty-four and very fortunate to have been selected for the executive director post. I like to believe that we outdid any other antipoverty program out there, because the young people we recruited were so receptive to being able to travel to new cities and states, and to receiving their training.

I also spent a lot of time working in the prison system with youthful offenders, which is where I found the bulk of candidates for the Job Corps. Although the Job Corps was not really set up to receive juvenile offenders, we argued that the system could do more good by supporting these young men and women, who had already done time in correctional facilities, and were at risk of being recidivists, if they didn't get help.

We fought, day and night, to get these kids a slot in job-training programs. Each week, I would gather up a group of working kids or local R&B groups, and go into the various correctional facilities in Manhattan at that time, such as "the Tombs," as we called them, and the Women's House of Detention in Greenwich Village, to recruit candidates for the Job Corps. We wanted to show these young people that there was a way to make a better life for themselves. We wanted to give them hope.

Sometimes, I took my younger brother, Bab'Brother, with me. He was skilled in karate, and would perform martial arts demonstrations for our potential recruits in prison to stimulate their interest in what we were offering. Our efforts were very effective, both in Harlem, and around the country. One famous Job Corps recruit was George Foreman (more about George later), who was trained in motor mechanics, down in Houston, Texas, I believe.

From time to time, I was required to go to court and speak on behalf of kids in trouble with the police. We could get their sentences reduced if we enrolled them in the Job Corps program, and sent them to a Job Corps facility. Many workers in the court system understood the concept, and supported it, because we had demonstrable success rates.

One particular young man, Arnold, who lived in our projects, was always getting into trouble, breaking into cars or stores, and playing on rooftops. You name it, Arnold would break into it, but he was really more mischievous than bad. One day, I got yet another call about Arnold. The police had caught him inside a store. I went down to "the Tombs," where Arnold had given my name as his counselor. We always kept our eye on the kids, and instructed them to call us if they found themselves in court or in a difficult situation, and needing our support.

"What happened this time?" I asked Arnold when I arrived. With a straight face, he explained the situation to me: "I was leaning against the store window when the glass broke," he said. "I was trying to get into the cash register to leave a note with my name and address so they could find me."

"If I tell a judge that story," I told Arnold, "he will have us both carted off to jail and thrown in the same cell."

Arnold was a remarkable young man with an amazing imagination. Later on, when I was involved in making a film called Black Caesar, I cast Arnold in the movie, and everybody loved him. Years later, I saw him on the street as I was going up to Harlem, and he called out to me. "Mr. Bailey, don't you remember me? This is your main man, Arnold."

"Oh no!" I said in mock horror. "Don't do this to me." Turns out that by then, Arnold was a grandfather. He had finished high school and worked with Westinghouse, repairing refrigerators and air conditioners, with the skills he had learned in the Job Corps. He had three kids and three grandchildren, all of whom went to college, I believe. It never ceases to amaze me that, if you believe in young people and persevere, the programs designed to help them can really work.

I remember many cases of young people who turned their lives around through the Job Corps. One young lady, who stands out, came from Texas; her name was Pat. When she was fifteen or so, Pat got into an argument with one of her pimp's other "wives", and she stabbed the girl to death. I found Pat in the Women's House of Detention, as she was waiting to be sentenced. She was beautiful, but you could tell that she had led a very rough life with no formal education, except what she had learned growing up on the streets. Pat knew of no other way to make money than to have a pimp, and to be one of his five "ladies," as they called themselves.

I worked with Pat for over a year in the Women's House of Detention, and she told me some horrendous stories, during my hour-long visits, and group counseling sessions with her. When she was very young, she had been abused and molested by male family members—father, uncles and brothers. She told me about people she had tried to knife or kill, but when I looked in her eyes, I saw that she was just a young girl, looking for direction; a person who really wanted to make a better life, but who didn't know the right way, and did not have the means to go about doing it.

I was very fortunate to convince the judge, presiding over her case, to give Pat another chance to have a normal life, in spite of the overwhelming evidence, which suggested that she could not be rehabilitated. "I have a strong belief that nobody is born rotten," I told the judge. "Sometimes bad circumstances get the best of a person. Just give her the chance to try our program." I told him about all our success stories over the years with Job Corps and HARYOU-ACT. The judge listened, and after examining our success rate with the recruits from the houses of detention, he released Pat into my custody.

As we walked out of the courthouse, Pat tapped me on the shoulder. "Mr. Bailey, where is your wallet?" she asked. I checked my coat. Sure enough, she had picked my pocket. "Just checking to make sure I still have the skills to do it," she said, laughing.

Pat didn't have a place to live, so my mother invited her to stay with us in Lincoln Projects. Two of the five brothers had already left home, so there was extra room. Pat liked sewing and had a real knack for it. She loved African textiles and music, and she was a great cook, who always helped my mom prepare dinner.

Bab'Brother used to practice his karate moves on Pat, and every time that she started acting up, Bab'Brother took her to the dojo (karate school), so that she could vent her frustrations, and let off steam in a safe environment. He taught her how to get her anger out in a positive way.

"What did you do to her?" Mom would ask whenever the pair came home from the dojo. "Just toughening her up a bit," Bab'Brother replied.

"She's a young lady, don't go beating up on her," my mother said, but Bab'Brother explained that, on the contrary, he was just teaching Pat the art of self-defense, in case someone attacked her with a knife or a gun.

Pat was a good student and earned her black belt in karate. She went on to marry a young man she met in the Job Corps. Her husband earned a Bachelor of Arts and a Master's Degree in Black Studies. He started teaching at a local university, and he eventually received a PhD from the University of Houston, where they now live. They have two children and Pat works quite a bit in her community with young people. She also has an African clothing store, and makes clothes on the side for kids who can't afford them.

The kids buy the fabric, Pat designs the garments, and then she teaches the kids how to sew them. I guess this is her way of giving back. I have been told by the people who know her in Houston that she is quite an inspiration to the young men and women in her community. I am very proud of her.

Twelve

The Commodores Years

"I went to the Joyful Noise performance of the Harlem Gospel Choir last night, at Sanders Theater in Cambridge, and it was absolutely fabulous!"
—**Nancy, Massachusetts**

Back when I was still at High School of Fashion Industries, I met a very popular liquor wholesaler in Harlem named Benny Ashburn. I was still living in Lincoln Projects and Benny lived in Lenox Terrace. My friends and I used to hang out at a restaurant in Lenox Terrace called 22 West, where all the liquor salesmen used to go for lunch. It wasn't a formal meeting; we recognized each other as people who belonged to the neighborhood, the way that New Yorkers always do. Benny was very outgoing, the type who would just walk up to you and begin a conversation. One day, he came over and started talking to us. It turned out that he had seen me around, and knew a lot of the same people I knew, including Ruthie Bowen.

Gradually, we developed a friendship, and eventually Benny, who was about eight years my senior, became my best friend. During this time, we used to attend a lot of the same social functions in Harlem, but it was not until 1968 that we began working together. The year before, Benny had called to tell me that he had seen a dynamite group, in Tuskegee, Alabama, called the Mighty Mystics. The group consisted of just three performers: William King on trumpet, Thomas McClary on guitar, and Lionel Richie on vocals and saxophone.

Benny had gone down to Alabama to attend the homecoming of his then girlfriend, at Tuskegee Institute, and had seen the Mighty Mystics playing at an amateur night contest, that was part of the homecoming celebrations.

Benny was very excited about the group. He wanted to get my opinion, and also my help in bringing the guys up to New York, to showcase them in the various nightclubs and ballrooms here. I told him that I would help him with the expenses, because the guys, who were pretty much penniless students, were forced, when they arrived in New York, to sleep on Benny's floor; I would go out to get them cheeseburgers and fries from McDonald's.

I introduced the group to a guy by the name of Pete McDougal, who owned a club in Harlem called Smalls Paradise. Pete's partner was Wilt Chamberlain, a famous basketball star. Pete said he would showcase the Mighty Mystics on Monday nights to see how well they could draw.

Smalls Paradise was very popular at the time and attracted a lot of the downtown crowd. Pete had several stars, including King Curtis, who performed there on a regular basis. The deal was that the Mighty Mystics, or the Commodores, as they were now known, would receive the money that people paid to come into the club (the door charge at that time was ten to fifteen dollars), and the club would get the bar sales. All the beautiful people from Harlem, and a lot of downtown people, used to frequent Smalls, so the high door charge was not a problem. The Commodores built up quite a following, all the while sleeping on Benny's floor. They did well enough for Pete to give them several nights a week, plus part of the proceeds from the bar, after he had met expenses.

This drill went on for over a year. Whenever they were on a school break, the Commodores would return to New York and perform at Smalls Paradise. Benny was still earning a very good living from his liquor wholesale business, and I was promoting shows at the Fifth Avenue Hotel, near Washington Square, which sadly was torn down some years ago. I first met Stevie Wonder and his brother, Calvin, in the hotel lounge, while they were staying there. Calvin told me that Stevie was there to work on an album, and I think he stayed for over a year. I also met Stevie's attorney, a strange guy called Johanan Vigoda, who was always busy, and seemed very fidgety with a short attention span. Perhaps trying to manage Stevie's business affairs made him that way.

While Benny was showcasing the Commodores at Smalls Paradise, he also booked them to perform at private functions, one of which, was an attorneys' convention. It was here that the Commodores made such an impression on Motown executive, Suzanne De Passe, that she hired them to be the warm-up band for the Jackson Five on a world tour. That tour was called Ninety-Nine Nights in Ninety-Nine Cities, although it went on to last for nearly three years, and gave the Commodores amazing arena experience.

Because it lasted so long, I was on and off that tour. Benny had not negotiated guaranteed money for the group, assuming that no Jackson Five dates would be cancelled. Benny wound up losing quite a bit of money, because when a date was cancelled, the Commodores, who were working for bare minimum, in exchange for the right to work on the tour, did not get paid. Moreover, the tour managers had to go to Motown executive, Ewart Abner, when they needed cash on the tour. Ewart refused to pay the Commodores for the days they had off, nor were they given a per-diem amount for daily living expenses. Benny would always tell me that Ewart was a guy who was born without a heart, because he watched the Commodores struggle with no per-diem for food or incidentals, on the off-days, and he would never try to help them.

All the same, the group learned to cope, and the tour gave them national exposure. Every night, the Commodores made it real hot for the Jackson Five, because they kept getting encores, and they were just the opening act. That made the group a real tough act for the Jackson Five to follow. Off stage, however, all the guys, in both acts, got along great.

The Commodores' first recording with Motown, an instrumental called "Machine Gun," was a big hit. As the group became more and more successful, with more album releases and supporting tours, I grew busy, too; sometimes on the tour, and sometimes on the road in advance of the tour, checking to see that the local promotion was going according to schedule. If it wasn't, I would call Benny to let him know, and Benny would call the local promoter. Benny was the "sixth" Commodore in a very real sense, since the money that the group earned was split evenly, six ways.

Benny will always be remembered, because he did a lot of work in the community, and he always made sure that the neighborhood kids got free tickets to the Commodores' shows, whenever they came back to New York. He never forgot his roots and it kept him very humble.

During breaks from touring with the Commodores, Benny, the group and I would drive, on the tour bus, up to Oak Bluffs on Martha's Vineyard. Benny's family had a small bed-and-breakfast complex up there called Shearer Cottages. At the end of a long tour, during the summers, we would all really look forward to some well-earned rest and relaxation in that peaceful environment.

Soon after we were married, I took Anna to stay in Oak Bluffs. I introduced her to Benny's cousin, Liz White, who ran the cottages for Benny's family at that time, and we visited Benny's grave, because he had died by then.

An artist, whom the Commodores had great respect for, was Bob Marley, who performed only one concert with them—at Madison Square Garden, in 1979. Sadly, he died soon after that show. He was a very religious and humble man, a Rastafarian. I saw him during sound check, joking with crew members and the Commodores, who treated him like the starring act, even though Bob was playing support, because the Commodores' record sales were higher than his.

Bob loved kids, and he had invited quite a few children backstage at Madison Square Garden, that night. His band was very friendly, with great positive energy that poured out of them at sound check, before the concert.

The most frequent opening act, on the Commodores' tours, was an all-girl band called the Emotions. All the girls were very nice and pleasant to work with, and they soon became for the Commodores, what the Commodores had been for the Jackson Five—a high-energy, exciting and hard act to follow.

Finally, in 1972, the Commodores were signed to MoWest, which was then Motown's new subsidiary, started after the label's move from Detroit to Los Angeles. Little did Motown know that they had just got their hands on what would be one of their biggest acts of the 1970s.

Benny's job managing the Commodores was very stressful and certainly did not enhance his health. In the early '80s, Lionel Richie began talking about leaving the group, and going out on his own, as a solo act. Benny told me that Lionel had decided to go in another direction and that he wished him well. I could tell, however, that it was taking a toll on Benny, because it felt to both of us, like a member of the family was leaving.

By this time, I was already removed from the group in so many ways, and pursuing my own promotions. The group was spending a lot of time in Los Angeles, while Benny and I were still based in New York, with Benny taking trips out to Los Angeles when he could.

On August 16, 1982, my dear friend, Benny Ashburn, died of a heart attack. We had just had dinner at my place; takeout from a local Chinese restaurant in the neighborhood called China Grill. We had been discussing the new projects we wanted to take on, including managing new talent, such as Alyson Williams who was Benny's secretary. This was not to be, because Benny died that night, after he got home to Lenox Terrace; he was only fifty-four. Alyson is now a successful jazz and R&B singer, and appears at the Blue Note in New York, from time to time.

Not long after Benny died, my own appetite for the star-studded entertainment world began to wane. After all, I had toured on and off with the Commodores, and with other notable performers, for over seventeen years, enjoying very good times on the road. By this time, I was jaded and ready for something new.

Thirteen

The Birth of the Harlem Gospel Choir

"Mr. Bailey, the Harlem Gospel Choir was magnificent! You are doing a great job with them. May God continue to bless you and the Choir."
—Phil, New Mexico

People sometimes ask me why I made the move, from working as a manager in the "glamorous" world of pop stars and entertainers, to managing a gospel choir. There were many reasons for the move. The biggest reason was that I just grew tired of that side of the entertainment industry, in general, and of the antics of inflated egos, in particular.

Slowly, over the years, disillusionment crept over me, as I witnessed more and more incidents that left me shaking my head and wondering just what I had gotten myself into. A few pivotal incidents helped push me in a different direction, in the direction of combining my love of music and performance, with my desire to serve something bigger than my own, or somebody else's, ego.

One night, on tour with a performer who shall remain nameless, and after a seventeen-hour-long flight from Sydney, Australia, to Los Angeles, I stumbled exhausted into bed, at the five-star hotel, that our entourage had checked into. Deep in sleep, I was awakened, by the ringing phone, next to my bed. "Yes?" I answered, groggy and exhausted.

"Fifty-fifty," my famous boss announced.

"Fifty-fifty what?" I asked.

SINGING GOD'S WORK

Allen's bedroom window, Abraham Lincoln Projects (third floor, last window on left)

Allen's mother, Rose Lee Bailey and grandson, Darryl

The New York Gems Basketball Team (Allen, far left, back row)

Allen Bailey

Allen (kneeling left front row) High School of Fashion Industries

Allen in slave costume for Aida at the Met

Allen with Jesse Jackson

SINGING GOD'S WORK

Allen with Shari Belafonte

Benny Ashburn

Allen with Coretta Scott King

Allen Bailey

The Choir with Bono, Senator Frist and his wife, at Rockefeller Center

Post concert, Arnez greets Hana from Japan

Our work continues for Feed the Children

SINGING GOD'S WORK

Kareem Abdul-Jabbar, formerly Lew Alcindor

Allen's father, George Bailey

Fun at the Lake House Retreat

Allen Bailey

The Choir with "Flying Dutchman," André Rieu

Lifting up the Choir with Sri Chinmoy

SINGING GOD'S WORK

New York Congressman, Charles Rangel, with Allen and Choir members

Allen with Job Corps kids

Allen with the Three Degrees

Allen with Chief Justice Arthur Goldberg

The Choir with Christopher Reeve at the Hole in the Wall Gang Camp

SINGING GOD'S WORK

The Choir at Sir Elton John's 60th birthday, Cathedral of St. John the Divine

Paul Newman with the Choir at the Hole in the Wall Gang Camp

Allen with Barack Obama, Apollo Theater, February, 2008

Allen with Amy Grant

Brian Cussen on stage with the Choir

"Fifty-fifty," was again the answer. We went back and forth, on this fifty-fifty track, till my sleep-deprived self managed to coax the problem out of my agitated employer. "My sheets are fifty percent cotton and fifty percent polyester," he said finally. This seemed unlikely, given the caliber of the hotel, but I played along. "What do you want me to do?" I asked.

"Get me a set of one-hundred-percent cotton sheets," he demanded.

"It's 3AM in downtown LA," I argued. "Where am I going to find a set of cotton sheets?"

"I want new cotton sheets—one hundred percent! Now!" came the answer.

With that, I dragged myself out of bed, and managed to summon a concierge, who made a few phone calls to other nearby five-star hotels, to help me find all-cotton sheets, and then arranged for housekeeping to make up a new bed for the boss. The boss was a man who had grown up dirt poor, sharing a bedroom with four siblings, and who, at one time, thought himself lucky to have sheets, even. But now, apparently, he could not sleep unless he was swaddled in the softest cotton weave.

I witnessed more of this same foolishness when a different performer, with whom I worked, repeatedly enforced the technical rider, which stipulated that he be served only yellow M&Ms in his dressing room. This meant that a grown person had to dig through a five-pound bag of M&Ms to extract only the yellow candies, and then discard the rest.

But, perhaps the straw that broke the camel's back, came when I was part of a team, touring with another pop superstar. He sent down instructions that, if any of the managers or crew passed him, we were to avert our eyes and not look at him. Has he deified himself? I asked myself. It was then I made the decision that if I was going to worship someone, it was going to be someone who wore a halo, and not a baseball cap. The die was cast, and I was ready to move towards something different, towards a more wholesome and rewarding life.

Again and again in the music business, I had marveled at how success and big money transformed performers, before my very eyes. Isolated by luxury and excess, they often seemed to forget that they were just flesh and blood creatures. Enabled by managers, who stipulated with whom they could, and could not, hang out, many of these artists forgot the people—the family and friends, who had supported them along the road to success. It is easy to forget that in the music business, you might be up one day, but the next day, you might be down. I realized that staying rooted in your community, with the people who loved you before you had money and fame, is key for survival and well-being. I was ready to make a move.

As a result of these realizations, I set out on a path that led to my founding the Harlem Gospel Choir in 1986, and fittingly, my inspiration came on the very first national holiday for Dr. King, held on his birthday, on January 15. I remember that on this day, we had just returned from church, and, as was usual on Sundays after church, we had headed over to the Cotton Club for gospel brunch. Oh, the pleasure in all that traditional black soul food: mac 'n' cheese, collard greens, fried chicken, corn on the cob and sweet potatoes. Today, the Harlem Gospel Choir is resident at B.B. King Blues Club in Times Square, where the club serves a soul-food buffet brunch, and where the Choir sings to a sold-out house, every Sunday. You might even see me there, directing the patrons in the buffet line.

But, back on that momentous Sunday in 1986, we were celebrating Dr. King's birthday, and the first national holiday in his honor, watching excerpts from his sermons and speeches on television. I remember hearing one reporter, passing around accolades about all the great things that Dr. King had accomplished. I listened, and focused on a particular clip, in which, Dr. King was claiming that it was possible for us all to do great things, because we all are capable of serving the Lord. This statement hit me hard, because right there and then, I realized that I could serve, that I was ready to serve, and I knew exactly how I wanted to do it.

Back in the 1980s, New York City tour operators had begun to bring busloads of tourists up to Harlem to experience the power of our choirs. At that time, Harlem was still not on the main tourist beat, and a tour bus provided a comfortable way for visitors, from around the world, to experience the inspirational music sung by Harlem's mass choirs.

This practice was good for our community, because the tour operators made money and donated a portion to our churches; the tourists got to see a very positive side of Harlem, and to experience the unique music of its gospel choirs, which nurtured incredible homegrown talent, right there in the community.

More and more, our churches began to open their doors to visitors from around the world, and it was often the case that these visitors would petition the church choirs to go on tour. "Can you come to my country or my community and perform for us?" visitors would ask. But fulfilling these requests didn't seem feasible. Choirs are typically very large, and it is both cumbersome and expensive, to take this kind of show on the road.

As I heard the requests keep coming in, however, I began to think that there was a way to do it. Instead of taking a mass choir of fifty singers and musicians on tour, I figured, why not whittle a touring choir down to a more manageable number, say nine singers and three musicians—keyboard, drums and guitar? This way, all the performers and equipment would fit in a single tour bus, and on-the-road expenses could be kept to a minimum, something that tour operators and host organizations always prefer. This approach is the cornerstone of our touring practices today.

By this time in my career, I was a seasoned tour and event coordinator; I certainly had the know-how, experience and contacts to take on such an initiative, and the timing was perfect. I was disgruntled with my life and my career, and so on that Sunday in 1986, on Dr. King's birthday, it all came together: the demand for a touring gospel choir from Harlem, my ability to make it happen, and inspiration from the words of Dr. King himself, which galvanized me into attempting the venture.

As the months went by, and I began to focus on what I wanted the choir's purpose to be, I realized that I wanted to unite a group of performers into a singing ministry, committed to Dr. King's dream of service and uniting peoples. I also wanted to bring about a better understanding of the African-American culture, especially as it relates to the Black Church, which is such an important institution in the black community, where church is not just a place of worship that we attend for services once a week, but is also a vibrant and integral part of our lives, where we go in times of happiness and stress. Church is open to us every day, and many nights, offering varied local community support activities, such as Sunday School, Youth Fellowship, Bible Study, church-sponsored entertainment evenings, and services on Friday night, on Saturday night, and up to three times on Sundays. I was a product of the Black Church, I had benefited immensely from it, and now, I wanted to give something back.

In forming our new touring choir, I began to audition, within the Harlem churches and various civic organizations, for the finest singers and musicians I could find. There was plenty of talent, and it was not difficult to pull it together into a single, unified, Harlem Gospel Choir that represented the spirit and the traditions of Harlem.

Over the years, there have been plenty of pretenders to the throne, but, while we are often imitated, we are never duplicated. Other choirs have tried to poach our name, and ex-Choir members have launched solo careers, as so-and-so of the Harlem Gospel Choir. We wish them well, as long as they succeed on their own merit. I believe that there is even a Harlem Gospel Choir of Japan! We choose not to waste time and energy trying to pursue and prosecute every trademark and copyright violation. There is only one world-famous Harlem Gospel Choir, and everybody knows it. Over the last twenty-three years, we have logged more than two million touring miles, fulfilling ongoing requests from fans worldwide to visit their countries and sing for them.

Along the way, I have learned the wisdom of Uncle Pigmeat's words: "It takes a team to build a dream." One big lesson I learned, early on, was NO HEADLINERS. Whenever we put a particularly talented performer out front and center stage, and place his or her name above the Choir's, as in "John Doe and the Harlem Gospel Choir," it simply does not work. How we structure the Choir has changed a great deal from 1986 to the present. Today there are no star turns. Most Choir members have an opportunity to sing solos, but the Choir is billed and performs as an ensemble, as a team; it's just better that way.

Over the years, many of the choir members who have come and gone, have been extremely religious people. They, like many others I meet, are often astonished to learn that, while I feel close to God, and still love to attend my old, childhood church, the Greater Refuge Temple in Harlem, I am not particularly religious. I talk to God, which is to say that I pray every day, and I try and listen to hear what He is saying back to me. I try not to ask for too much, working instead on cultivating the attitude of gratitude, and the belief that, with God in charge, everything is going to work out okay. It works for me, because I have to say that most of the time my life is filled with peace and happiness.

Managing worldwide tours is hectic and tiring, but I am fortunate that our brand of music is uplifting to audiences, and rewarding for us; we see ourselves more as a ministry than as pure entertainment. Our ministry is to sing God's work with performances that bring hope and inspiration to global audiences. At the end of every concert, I watch people leave the auditorium, or whatever venue we are in, with big smiles on their faces. And because we are a nonprofit organization, we have been able to raise a great deal of money and awareness for children's charities, worldwide.

The Choir has never signed with a big record label, and yet for twenty-three years, we have worked constantly and enjoyed huge international and local success. Labels have approached us to make a record, and to include more "cross-over" music. My answer is always the same: "We don't mind crossing over, it's just that we are
        TAKING THE CROSS WITH US!"

Fourteen

How the Other Half Lives

"I saw you at Night of the Proms in Antwerp, and I must say you were all fantastic! The performance went right to my heart!!"
—**Sarah, Belgium**

    As a hungry child, growing up in the projects of Harlem, I didn't know what life had in store for me as an entertainment manager, and later, as the founder of a touring ministry that would take us to a star-studded gala like Elton John's sixtieth birthday party. But I did know that as I began to come of age, and make a little spending money from my various jobs, the finer things in life began calling to me.

    As I have already said, I was captivated by the images that I saw on the pages of the popular lifestyle magazine, *Town and Country,* and often fantasized about what it would feel like to be so well off. I think that these types of fantasies are common in poor kids growing up in a ghetto. After I had paid my mom out, I was always looking to save the money I had left over to buy this magazine, which cost a whopping seven dollars at the time. No matter; I shelled out the cash, because I was so intrigued with how white, especially rich, white people lived.

    I remember that when I was a small child, my dad would set me on his knee to ride the bus, downtown. We would get off at Fifth Avenue to stare at all the fancy shops that looked like wonderlands. Mannequins, outfitted in expensive clothes, stood in the windows of Saks Fifth Avenue and Bergdorf Goodman, while jewels shimmered in the windows of Harry Winston and Tiffany's. Cabs picked up, and dropped off, exclusive visitors and guests at the Plaza Hotel, right there next to Central Park, where people strolled or took carriage rides. It was a far cry from my world uptown in Harlem. After the rattrap we lived in, it just boggled my mind to see those well-heeled white folks, stepping out, living the good life, and shopping on Fifth Avenue.

In the early years, as we worked to get the concept of the Harlem Gospel Choir off the ground, it was touch and go. Anna and I worked, day and night, trying to secure bookings and tours. We had to take all kinds of jobs on the side to make ends meet.

I found that limo driving was a job that put extra money in my pocket, and gave me the flexibility I needed to stay focused on building the Choir's presence and reputation. I started a small limo service called Luxury Transportation for Less, a business that I could fall back on over the next few years, until the Choir took off. Almost immediately, the limo business began to do well. Work came mostly from word-of-mouth referrals, including plenty of bookings from rock groups that came into town to perform; I never had to advertise.

Working as a limo driver, I indulged in people-watching, and was able to get a closer look at the rich white folks who had so intrigued me when I was a kid. One couple I met, Roy and Mary Anderson, were not only extremely wealthy, but also very fine people, and stand out in my mind. Roy Anderson initially made his money, during the Second World War, from owning ships that delivered oil back and forth to the army. He knew and was friendly with both the Niarchos and Onassis families. Roy met Mary when she was working as a secretary. They fell in love, were married, and remained inseparable for the next seventy-five years.

One day, I received a call from another car service, saying that they needed help to drive a very demanding customer called Mary Anderson. If I could put up with her, they said, they were willing to outsource the account to me. The Andersons lived in the River House on Manhattan's East Side, along with the Rockefellers, the Kissingers, and the rest of the who's who of Manhattan. They had bought their apartment, in Kissinger House, for seventy-five thousand dollars in cash, back in 1950, and it was worth in the region of twenty million dollars, when Mary died, in 2008.

Despite her idiosyncrasies, Mary was an amazing woman; always impeccably dressed, if only to go shopping, or to run the smallest errand.

The car service that gave me the account told me to be sure to pad the bill before I gave it to them. "Mrs. Anderson won't even notice," they said. That didn't sit right with me. I had only a modest income at the time, but I was not a thief, so the first time I submitted a bill to the service, I was careful to mention to Mary that it was for two hundred dollars. This amount turned into six hundred dollars by the time Mary received the bill. Even she thought that three hundred percent was too much of a mark-up, so she asked me to work for her and take on the account directly. I began to chauffeur Mary around, and what I saw was like watching *Town and Country* magazine come alive, before my very eyes.

    I chauffeured the Andersons to a constant round of Broadway plays, exclusive restaurants and fancy dinners. Roy and Mary used to flee New York every winter. Eventually, grown bored with wintering in Palm Beach, they began, instead, to rent a suite of rooms at the Sheraton Royal Hawaiian in Honolulu, every winter. A few days before they arrived at the hotel, the staff would remove the usual hotel furnishings, and replace them with the couple's own furniture that was stored there for them. Mary knew how much I loved hearing her tell stories about that Royal Hawaiian suite. "You raise the money to get to Hawaii," she used to tell me, "and I'll let you stay in the suite for nothing." It was a great offer, but one that I never got the chance to take the great lady up on.

    I remember driving Mary to Harry Winston jewelers; the exclusive store would also send someone over to give Mary a private showing, if she did not feel well enough to drive to Fifth Avenue. Mary would spend up to a million dollars or more on jewels at one time. A buying spree like this was almost an annual event. Then, every six months or so, she would schedule an appointment to sell pieces from her collection back to Harry Winston, pieces that might have even gone up in value.

    One of Mary's friends was Gloria Vanderbilt, who also lived in the River House. One time, Mary told me, Gloria was dating the renowned black bandleader, Bobby Short, who was, at that time, performing nightly at Bemelmans Bar, at the Carlisle Hotel. Even so, Mary reported, a doorman at the River House had the nerve to tell Mr. Short to take the service entrance.

    Most of Mary's friends were as wealthy or wealthier than she was. I remember that another one, who lived in the River House, was the chairman of the pharmaceutical company, Bristol Meyers. This group of friends thought nothing of spending up to $1,500 for dinner at some exclusive local eatery.

As Roy became very sick, Mary would call me to ferry him back and forth to Lenox Hill hospital. When he became too frail to walk, I would pick him up and carry him, instead of putting him in a wheelchair. The Andersons had given millions of dollars to Lenox Hill Hospital in New York City, so that Roy could have a private room reserved for his use, there. He could be very demanding, especially after he lost his sight, which served to heighten his other senses. The hospital staff would try to ignore him, but he could always sense when I was there.

Mary became a lifelong friend and a huge fan of the Choir, and it thrilled her to watch our growing success. She was always good to Anna and me, occasionally treating us to extraordinary dinners at exquisite restaurants. I did meet many of her family, who were very nice, but it was very sad to me that most of the people whom Mary had taken care of and written checks for, did not show up at her funeral, or during the whole time that she was sick and in need of comfort.

I will always have fond memories of Mary's kindness and generosity. She showed me how the other half lives, and it was an amazing experience, and a real education, to talk to her, and to drive her around. One time, I called her up from the car. "I'm stuck in traffic and running late," I told her.

"Well, don't take too long," she said. "I'm ninety-six years old."

During her last years, Mary's old body began to fail and "let her down," as she put it. During one hospital stay at Lenox Hill, she had to share a room with another patient, as there were no private rooms available to her. Since she had donated a private room to the hospital, Mary was annoyed, and when I visited her there, she would quip to me: "The next time I donate a private room to this outfit, remind me to get the key!"

Fifteen

America's Own Paul Newman

"We wish you much blessing from our Lord. With love."
—Renata and George, Czech Republic

    From the great Pigmeat Markham, I learned that it takes a team to build a dream. From the incomparable Dr. Martin Luther King, I learned that the path to happiness and freedom comes by being in service to others, and in a spirit of uniting peoples. From another great humanitarian, whom, sadly, we lost, in 2008—Mr. Paul Newman, I learned powerful lessons about why the best use of success is to channel it into helping others, rather than simply squandering it on self-gratification.

    "Shameless self-promotion for the greater good," was one of Paul Newman's mottos. It is widely known that through his family's charities, including Newman's Own Foundation, which sells Newman's Own food products, Paul and his family raised, by some estimates, over $215 million for charities, worldwide. One of Paul's best-known endeavors is the string of Hole in the Wall Gang Camps for seriously ill children, which he started in the town of Ashford, in his and Joanne's home state of Connecticut.

    The Harlem Gospel Choir has performed several times for the kids at the original Hole in the Wall Gang Camp, and there is no other concert quite like it for us. When you enter the camp, in this picturesque little town, you are immediately impressed by how beautifully designed and maintained the compound is. The wild-west theme is played out with cabins, and statues of wooden bears, and a big Indian totem pole that capture a kid's imagination. The staff and volunteers, many of them college kids, are dedicated to the children, who themselves, are nothing less than inspirational.

    Any visitor to the camp can see that there is always lots of singing and chanting, and dancing of the Hole in the Wall Gang mambo, which seems to keep everyone's energy and spirits up. The kids get to play outdoors in this beautiful setting, and to take part in activities, including arts, drama and performance. I have been told that after the Choir's performances, certain kids have stolen our moves for their own acts, but I guess that's okay with us.

The camp has a beautiful theater, complete with a foyer and balcony, which is where camp performances take place. During our show, it is usual for us to always bring audience members onstage to sing and dance with us. It is a particular joy to do this at the camp. Some of the kids are often too sick to come up on stage, and others are forced to leave early to receive medication and treatment. Those who are able, however, throw themselves into the concert, and they take the stage by storm to sing and dance, and to shout that yes, with the Lord, anything is possible; miracles are possible, and healing is possible, even for those who are at the camp after hospitals have given up on them.

It is a very sad encounter, but if you ever witness a terribly ill child, you will understand the meaning of grace. These special children are fully present in the moment, and as long as they have the strength, they radiate hope and happiness. It hurts your heart, inspires and amazes you, all at the same time, to see them grab the moment, and live it.

It was on our first visit to the camp that Paul Newman, himself, was our host in escorting the Choir around, and showing them various places of interest. Our tour was interrupted by a quick visit with the kids, who showed us a number that they had been rehearsing. Paul later mentioned to me that he was a great fan of the Choir, and that he and Joanne were so happy that we had accepted their invitation to perform for his special kids.

For over fifty years of marriage, Paul and Joanne kept a low profile, committed to their craft, their family, their community and their inspirational charities. I know that they enjoyed a wonderful time with the kids they helped, and received from them, as much as they gave.

At my first meeting with Paul, I called him Mr. Newman, because I felt it was too familiar to do otherwise, but he insisted that I call him Paul. Each year now, the camp calls us to come back, and we accept, because it is just not possible to say no. As we walk around, we see how camp personnel keep Paul's special kids busy with all kinds of activities and games to keep their minds off of their more serious problems. The same holds true for all of his camps. I later had an opportunity, while I was in Ireland, to visit one of their Hole in the Wall Gang camps, and I found there, the same commitment to children, who are fighting terrible diseases.

On the evening of our visit with Paul, he and Joanne hosted a gala affair with celebrities and stars from Broadway and film, including Chita Rivera, Amy Grant and Christopher Reeve. We were scheduled to perform, and there was also an auction, so we had brought along Harlem Gospel Choir t-shirts, tour jackets and other paraphernalia to auction off.

Earlier in the day, singer Amy Grant had approached the Choir, and asked to perform with us. Amy is a great gospel singer herself, so we call her "blue eyed soul". We were very excited to sing a number with her called "Jesus Is Love," a Lionel Richie song. We had a wonderful time, and hopefully, one day, we will get another chance to sing with her. We also had a photo shoot with Paul, and Joanne took the pictures with some sort of special camera.

During our visit, I mentioned to Paul that I truly admired his ability to organize such a meaningful way to help children, and I expressed how one day I hoped to achieve something similar: to bring kids from inner-city New York into another environment to show them a different way of living. I asked Paul if he thought it would be possible to do what he had done on a smaller scale. "Well," he said, "you gotta start somewhere."

Several years later, I bought a piece of property in the Poconos of Pennsylvania, an ideal spot to carry out my idea for a retreat, where Choir members' kids can come and have fun. In our new lake house, there, we are able to accommodate as many as ten children, who can come visit, and discover what it's like to fish, row a boat, mountain climb and just enjoy the area.

July 4, 2009, was a beautiful day, and the grand opening of Lake House. We had a blast. My family came; many of the Choir members brought their kids, and we all enjoyed a wonderful barbecue with a lovely sunny day, in what was otherwise, a very wet summer. Everyone wrote or called afterwards to say what a good time they had had. You cannot imagine what it was like for the kids to come to a place like that, to run around and swim, and enjoy the pool and the lake, and to have our dog, Max, chase them.

I must say, though, that country living does take some getting used to. Coming from a New York City apartment, where the building superintendent fixes everything for you, it's quite an adjustment to live in a house, where you are responsible for all the repairs. I realize that I am a city person, and used to falling asleep to the sound of garbage trucks banging, and to police sirens blaring. This is a far cry from Lake House, where the chirping crickets put you to sleep, and the morning birdsong wakens you.

I have dedicated one of the rooms at the house to Paul Newman. We are in the process of painting it, and putting up pictures of our visit with Paul and his special kids, so that whenever I walk by it, I will be inspired. In time, I would like to establish an even more expansive Harlem Gospel Choir Retreat, including a log cabin and a vegetable garden, where kids can enjoy the outdoors, and where we can invite the friends we have made while touring abroad.

I always tell Choir members how lucky we are to travel the world, to meet people, and to make so many friends from such different cultures. A formal retreat would be a place where we could invite our overseas friends to come, and to receive good impressions of America, of African-Americans and of Harlem. Just a small effort towards Dr. King's dream of uniting peoples, and inspired, in part, by Mr. Paul Newman.

Sixteen

Rumble in the Jungle: Ali Versus Foreman

"The Choir is incredible and raised the roof to say the least. I did not sit down all night and couldn't have asked for a better time."
—Claire, Northern Ireland

    I first became involved with Muhammad Ali in the 1970s. His trainer, a guy by the name of Drew Bondini, was dating a girl who lived in my building. Over the years, Drew and I became friends. At that time, Drew was corner man for Ali, who had just won a couple of major fights. Drew was also Ali's friend and spiritual counselor of sorts. He had a whole repertoire of philosophical quotes, and he would feed these to Ali during their training sessions. I think that Drew might have been the inspiration behind some of Ali's most famous rhymes, such as "Float like a butterfly and sting like a bee." Ali would always touch Drew's head for good luck, just before a fight.
    One time, Lee Wade, who was a close friend of Ali's, and I, went to Ali's training camp in Deer Lake, Pennsylvania, not far from Allen Town. Helping out around the cabin there gave me a good workout. I used to get up at 5AM to chop firewood for the huge fireplaces that were in each of the cabin's rooms, and boy was it tough, because you really had to know what you were doing with that axe. I was in my early thirties by then, and I thought I was in pretty good shape, until Ali made us all look bad.
    Ali had sparring partners train with him at the camp, and he had hired a wonderful chef by the name of Alma, who was amazing. She cooked with fresh veggies, and boiled them in the well water, so the food was delicious.

Alma always told me to stay away from fried foods.

Ali ate a special diet of vegetables and protein. In the morning, he would have ten eggs, bacon, grits; you name it and Alma could make it. Then Ali would go for a run. What fascinated me about these runs was that he would wear combat boots. We tried to keep up with him in our sneakers, but we could not catch him, and Ali would taunt us. "I can't believe you guys are so out of shape," he would yell over his shoulder as we ate his dust. I remember being completely amazed by the fighter's discipline to follow his grueling regimen. Every morning, without fail, I would hear him climb out of bed. "Are you all staying in bed or working out?" he would yell.

At that time, Ali somehow or other took a liking to Don King, and made Don his promoter. My associate, Lloyd Price, was very close to Don King, who had just gotten out of jail after a little bit of trouble. I guess that, in the past, Lloyd had done favors for Don, who did not forget the good turns, because he tapped Lloyd to handle all the entertainment for the big fights. They would ask me to arrange for black models to be present, ringside, at Ali's fights, to act as ring girls, and hold up the signs that announce each round. I also booked models to attend promotional parties and receptions for corporate sponsors, which was easy, because, after the model tours I had managed, I still had a wide circle of friends who were models.

During this time, I was still working with Benny Ashburn and the Commodores. Benny was also helping to manage and finance some of my others projects, as well as managing several boxers himself, including Eddie Mustafa. Eddie also trained at Deer Lake in Pennsylvania. When Don King asked Lloyd Price to book entertainment for the upcoming "Rumble in the Jungle" contest, between Ali and George Foreman, Lloyd, in turn, asked me to help, because he was so busy. And that's how I became fortunate enough to arrive ringside at one of the greatest boxing matches of the twentieth century.

The Rumble in the Jungle was scheduled to take place in September 1974, in the Mai 20 Stadium, in Kinshasa, Zaire, now the Democratic Republic of Congo. It was one of Don's first ventures as a professional boxing promoter, and he persuaded both Ali and Foreman to sign separate contracts, saying that they would box for him, if he could secure a five-million-dollar payout for the fight.

Don did not have this much money, so he had to find a sponsor, or in this case, a country, to put up the cash. Zaire's flamboyant President Mobutu Sese Seko, eager for the publicity such a high-profile happening would bring, requested that the fight be held in his country. Mobutu was on the receiving end of a lot of bad press at that time, and he was convinced that this international event would bring positive world attention to his country, and help to boost tourism in Zaire. To round out Mobutu's sponsorship, Don put together a consortium of promoters: a Panamanian company called Risnelia Investment; the British company, Hemdale Film Corporation; Video Techniques Incorporated of New York; and of course, Don King Productions.

For the entertainment line-up, I began reaching out to all the people we had worked with in the past, and we were able to put together a wonderful group of musicians: the Pointer Sisters, James Brown, Bill Withers, the Spinners, Etta James and a group called Fanya All-Stars, a Latin group led by Johnny Pacheco.

When it came time to fly everyone to the Congo, however, life became more complicated. Don King had chartered a plane to fly the entertainers on World Airways from New York, JFK, directly to Kinshasa. The airline staff informed us when we were all on the plane, but still at the gate, that the weight of the passengers would have to be more evenly distributed for such a long flight. The staff then began juggling seating and baggage to even out the loads. Some of us had to move, but James Brown refused to change his seat, and gave us all a hard time. In the end, we couldn't get him to budge, so Bill Withers volunteered to move all around, until the loads were balanced, and we eventually took off.

We arrived in Kinshasa at 4AM local time. When we landed, the ground crew unloaded our belongings, and put everything on the tarmac. James Brown had very expensive Louis Vuitton luggage, and when he saw it lying on the dirty tarmac, he got very upset. "Take my stuff and put it inside!" he yelled. "Take my stuff and put it inside!"

Next, we were handed an itinerary for the week, and learned that we were staying at the Inter-Continental Hotel, Kinshasa. Once again, James Brown made a stink. He didn't want to stay at the hotel and demanded that the staff find him alternative accommodations. The Inter-Continental was fine for everyone else, so we all checked in, and got settled. Ali and Foreman were already there. They had made a point to come much earlier to begin training under local conditions, and to become acclimated to the hot tropical humidity.

We were all tired and miserable after our twelve-hour flight, and all we wanted to do was sleep, but at the same time, it was my first time in Africa, so I also wanted to explore. Being there was such a special experience that I don't have the words to express what it all meant, except to say, that it felt like I was finally coming home. In the faces of the airport staff, I saw the faces of my family and friends. It was very moving and uplifting, despite the bone-shaking weariness I felt, after such a long journey.

In the days that followed our arrival, I took to walking around Kinshasa with Ali's father, Cassius Clay Sr., with Bill Withers, and with some of the sound and light crew, who were with the London-based company, ShowCo.

The local people invited us out to their manufacturing shops and warehouses, where they tried to sell us locally made arts and crafts, at inflated prices that we haggled over, until we got them down. I soon got the hang of how to bargain with them. Because the merchants didn't understand our American English, whenever they quoted a price, I made an exaggerated facial expression to show them that it was too high, or I pitted them against each other: "You want ten Zairians?" I would exclaim to a seller. "That guy over there is only asking for three!" In this way, I managed to amass quite a collection of African statues and masks, that, sadly, have disappeared, over the years, claimed by family and friends. Today I am left with very few souvenirs to remind me of that special trip.

As we walked around the city, I noticed that the locals were very interested in our being African-Americans, and they wanted our Levi 501 jeans, which, I guess, were prized there, but scarce. The natives all spoke English with a French accent, and, since the best educated among them worked for the government, we were surrounded, most of the time, by very well-spoken people. They were Muslim, and I remember Ali praying, and going to the mosques there. They were wonderful people with a refreshing local philosophy—"No problem" was the catch phrase in Kinshasa.

Apart from temper tantrums and bruised egos, there was a much larger problem with the fight plans: some how or another, during his training,

George Foreman had pulled a muscle, and been cut. He needed time to recover, so the fight, which had been scheduled to happen in September, had to be postponed until October 30. Not only was everyone disappointed, but there was also a negative ripple effect on our tour, because none of the entertainers we had booked wanted to stay in Zaire for another month. As a result, some of us remained, while others were flown home, and then flown back again, a few days before the rescheduled concert was to take place.

Throughout October, training continued for both fighters. The entertainers did not really belong to either camp, so we all hung out together, and kept to ourselves, given that we did not have much in common with anyone else. Some performers were pretty eccentric in their habits: Etta James had a physical therapist with her, because she had a serious back problem; James Brown surrounded himself with "yes" people, and tried to completely control his environment. He was a wonderful man, but he wanted what he wanted, when he wanted it, because, as he often pointed out, he was James Brown. And in Africa, James was like a king, because the people there loved his music. In fact all the performers were very popular there.

Naturally, there was a lot of speculation about which fighter would win and why. Foreman was the world champion, and Ali was the contender, having lost the heavyweight championship some years earlier. Foreman was younger, bigger and more powerful, while Ali was considered faster and smarter.

We were all staying in the same hotel, and we had to be careful about meeting up in the halls, because Ali's people disliked Foreman's people, and vice versa. Even going down to breakfast in the morning could be contentious. Every time Ali bumped into Foreman, he started running his mouth, and it always seemed that he had ten more things to say to George, about how he was going to knock him out, in which round, and with how many hits. George never answered back, because he didn't pay Ali any mind. The two were not friends, and we had to make sure that the training sessions were at different times, because even their staff didn't get along.

Ali planned his training times carefully to avoid mosquitoes, to clear routes for his runs outside, or to book training equipment, so he could work out indoors. Ali had no fear of being kidnapped, because should anything have happened to the fighter, Mobutu was a dictator, and would have basically shut down Zaire.

Ali was the people's favorite. The whole country was rooting for him, because George was viewed as the big, bad, mean fighter. But George had just knocked out Joe Frazier, and he was the gamblers' favorite, as they laid bets on who would win. George was continually showboating—showing off his muscles, which confounded the locals who could not relate to displays like this. By contrast, Ali raised money for local children's charities, and took time out to visit a local hospital. Whenever local kids wanted an autograph, he stopped and made sure he signed for every child. He truly loved children. There was a chant that was sung all around Zaire, leading up to and during the fight: "Ali combaya!" which means "Ali, come by here!"

I believe that Ali's father, Cassius Clay Sr., was a big ingredient in his son's success. He taught Ali to believe that he was greatest, but always to remember to give back. "Put in your head that no one can beat you and believe it," Cassius Sr. told his son. Cassius Sr. was a character himself. I remember him telling me how it is always possible to tell the exact age of a woman just by looking at her hands. "Allen, no matter what they do to their face or body," he said, "you can always tell their age by their hands." Cassius had another son, Rudy, the complete opposite of Ali. Rudy was Ali's corner man, and he did not like attention or "nonsense," as he called it. Cassius told me that he accepted Ali's changing his name from Cassius Clay to Muhammad Ali. "Ali is his own man," he said. "He's entitled to believe what he wants to believe."

Ali came from a good, stable home in Louisville, Kentucky. With the first decent money he made, he bought his mother, Odessa, a Cadillac. And Ali took his father everywhere he wanted to go. Cassius knew that Ali had a lot of hangers-on, keen to take advantage, and "invest" Ali's money for him. The father did not appreciate the fact that everyone, but Ali himself, was getting rich off his hard work. Cassius always had a word of advice for his son, little tips that he passed on, and he taught him the magic tricks that Ali used to delight the kids he visited in hospitals.

In the days before the fight, Cassius Sr. and I, continued our walks around Kinshasa. "Allen, look carefully, and you can see your ancestors," he would tell me. I took notice, and became very aware that many of these people, whom we saw in the streets, did resemble friends back in Harlem. I felt as though I were actually coming face-to-face with my roots.

Cassius Sr. had so much wonderful wisdom to give me and I just soaked it all in. "Let me tell you why the sky is blue and why the birds fly," he would say, and then he would be off, explaining the world, according to Cassius Clay Sr. It was easy to see where Ali acquired many of his traits. Sometimes, I would watch the two of them together. Ali was always very respectful, leaning down, so that his father could whisper advice into his ear. Whatever Cassius told him, it must have worked, because Ali always had a smile on his face.

The weather was sweltering—130 degrees in Kinshasa, forcing the fighters to rest up before their face-off. Don King continually held press meetings to hype the fight. A consummate salesman and promoter, he really worked at selling the match. News organizations were inclined to cancel the airing of this worldwide event, because of the postponement, due to Foreman's injury, but the fight broadcast was too important to Don, and he fought hard to make sure that it would come off.

Finally, the day of the fight dawned, and it was very hectic from the get-go. General admission tickets to the pre-fight concert were free to the local population. I was given ten front row house seats, which I gave to the hotel workers who had looked after us—the maids and the kitchen workers; they all wanted a ticket.

I had spent each morning, during the week before the concert, at the stadium, watching ShowCo. sound and light technicians set up the stage for the concert. I was amazed at how they could rig, light and mike a 60,000-seat stadium, and make it seem as intimate as if you were sitting in Madison Square Garden, which has only 18,000 seats. I've always had so much respect for the people behind the scenes, who make live events happen, and who, generally, don't get any credit. I'm amazed at how they can toil day after day, and I enjoy watching the unselfishness of these workers, as they help each other out. I continually remind the Choir of how important it is to work together as a team, and to put personal differences aside for the good of the show and the audience.

On the Ninety-nine Shows in Ninety-nine Nights Commodores tour, our sound and light guys made everything work, every single night, without fail; setting up in the late morning, and breaking down early the next morning, before driving to the venue scheduled for that day.

As I watched the stadium preparations, in the days before the fight, I could hear people yelling and screaming: "Did you get his stuff? Did you get his grease?" It was chaos, complete chaos, and I didn't think the fight was going to happen, because every time I turned around, something else seemed to have gone missing. Whenever anyone complained to nearby African workers, they would typically just shrug. "Well, it's Africa, so what do you want?" they said, and then they would smile and say, "No problem," and keep on working, no sweat. They were just wonderful people.

The pre-fight celebration, in both camps, began early in the day with both sides all fired up about their respective champion, and all the handlers and production crew ready to declare victory for their favorite, right then and there. The posturing was everywhere, as I bumped into people from George's party, who looked at me and sneered.

We left the hotel early in the afternoon for the concert, and Mobutu had engaged his personal army to escort us to the stadium, through streets that were lined with crowds of excited, cheering people. Early evening, and the concert got underway, and it was a rousing success, but afterwards, the fight started late, because there were problems syncing the broadcast with the United States. I was sitting in the third or fourth row back, when I saw George make his way through the stadium, and out to the ring, to the pulsing beat of an R&B tune. He looked young, fit, massive and in top form. Ali came out next, and I don't recall what music was playing, because all I remember thinking was that Foreman was going to kill him!

The bell signaled the start of round one. In no time, Ali's trainer was furious, screaming direction at Ali, who was bouncing around the ring too much. "It's all right, I got it under control," Ali shot back. "I'm just blocking the shots and laying on the ropes." I could hear Rudy, Ali's brother and corner man, yelling, too: "Get out of the way or he's going to knock your head off!" But Ali was too busy aggravating George to hear. "Can't you hit harder than that?" he taunted his opponent.

After a while, George seemed to be getting more and more rattled, and that's exactly what Ali wanted; he was making George lose his cool and forget his fight plan. And Ali was tiring his opponent, by leaning on George, who then had to support Ali's weight. Ali's tactics worked. Suddenly, in the eighth round, it was over as Ali delivered a devastating combination: a left hook, followed by hard right, that felled a fatigued Foreman. Against all odds, Muhammad Ali had regained the heavyweight title from a younger, stronger George Foreman.

The next day, a triumphant Ali ate breakfast, and walked around the hotel with neither a bruise, nor a scratch on him. "I am still pretty," he gloated. "I am still pretty." Later, he did an interview with Howard Cosell, the number-one sports announcer in the United States at that time. Cosell and Ali usually kept up a running patter in interviews, continually jibing at each other, but after Ali lost his heavyweight title, because he had refused the draft, Howard spoke out in defense of the fighter, who, in turn, always respected him for the gesture.

I've always believed that Muhammad Ali is an inspirational role model for our young people. He came, as I did, from very humble beginnings, but rose to the top of his profession, and held to his beliefs at huge cost. In the interview, after Ali won the championship, when Howard Cosell asked him if he thought he was worth five million dollars, Ali's answer stumped the commentator. "If I'm not worth five million dollars, and I am the champion of the world," Ali told Cosell, "then what do you think you are worth?" Howard had no answer; he just smiled.

Seventeen

A Mighty Talent: The Singers of the Harlem Gospel Choir

"I went to your performance at the Lebanon Opera House and you were AMAZING!"
—Chris, New Hampshire

Whenever we audition new singers for the Choir, we often find exceptionally talented vocalists, but for some reason, their performances do not always move us. Gospel has to be sung from the heart if its message of hope and inspiration is to reach the audience; mere vocal technique and prowess, as admirable as these might be, are not enough. We do not allow any preaching in our concerts, and many of our audiences understand little or no English, so we can share our message only through the power of the music itself.

This is why it is a blessing, when we audition wonderful singers, who have both vocal and emotional presence on stage, to reach an audience in a powerful and positive way, and sometimes, these singers bring a new song to our set list. This is how we added the song, "The Lord Is High Above the Heavens," to our set.

One Sunday, at the B.B. King Blues Club, where the Choir performs weekly, we auditioned a wonderful young man named Horace. Tall and shy offstage, he bounded onto the stage with a new song. We liked both him and the song so much, that we hired him as our vocal director, for a three-month tour to Europe, with Night of the Proms, and we made "The Lord Is

High Above the Heavens," the opening song on most of our tours. Everyone always notices how quiet Horace is offstage, and how animated and energetic he is onstage; the difference is quite remarkable.

Occasionally, we find a singer who is just so talented that he or she can sing anything, after hearing it only once. We work with one of these singers every Sunday, at B.B. King's Blues Club, for our gospel brunch. Her name is Tiona and she manages to sing the same song, "How Excellent," every week, while still making each performance sound new and like a heartfelt testimony. Despite her great talent, Tiona avoids the trap of diva-style behavior, and often helps other singers refine their songs, when she is on tour. We always count it as a great blessing, when we find singers who are willing and able to sing any song perfectly, with little or no rehearsal.

Sometimes, we work with some lovable rascals—very talented singers and musicians who like to push the envelope in small ways. We had one musician who was the epitome of this. His name was Paul, and he always began the tour by arriving at the airport, as late as possible. His excuse was always that he had to drive from Newburgh, New York, and that it took him extra time to navigate the traffic.

Once we were at JFK, about to check in to British Airways for our flight to London, when we were met by a gate agent, who informed us that our flight had been cancelled, but that, if we were all there, she would put us on the next flight out, which departed an hour later. Because of the time it would take to move us to the front of the check-in line, and then rush us through security, this option would only be possible if we were all present. "We're still waiting for one more," Anna explained.

"I'm sorry," said the gate agent, "you go now, or you have to wait for the last flight out." Paul finally arrived, looking cool in his sunglasses, and no one would talk to him, especially the seasoned travelers, who had arrived early to ensure they were on time, and who had already been at the airport for almost three hours.

Some of our musicians are very clothes conscious and, one in particular, has a reputation for very flamboyant dressing. He wears his hair long, and often arrives at rehearsal in matching shoes, pants, jacket and hat—all in red or blue or green leather. Once in Buenos Aires, our group was meeting in the hotel lobby, before going on to the venue for sound check, when our snappy dresser came in, all excited. He was wearing a new leather suit and matching leather hat in butter yellow. Since he is over six feet tall, he really stood out in a city, where there are few African-Americans, and where leather suits are not a major fashion item. Exclaiming over his new butter-yellow leather suit, he described how people were staring at him as he walked out of the tailor's, and back to the hotel, in his new clothes. "Let me tell you," he said, "as I crossed the street, I stopped traffic."

"I bet you did!" one of our singers quipped, and everyone cracked up.

Besides loving clothes, this performer is also a very talented pianist. On tour, whenever we can't find him in his room, we check the hotel lobby, to see if he is at the piano, playing classical music for the enjoyment of the hotel guests and staff. I think his playing is one of the reasons why the Choir is welcome in fine hotels all over the world.

Another lovable rascal was Mother Alice. We called her Mother Alice, because she was the oldest in the touring choir, and everyone respected her. Mother Alice has an amazing tenor voice with a huge range, and she can sing gospel and jazz, in a truly powerful way. Mother Alice is also big and tall, and she loves to break the cardinal rule of all vocalists: no dairy before a performance. Dairy food produces mucus in the throat and nasal passages, and it is cold, which can cause the vocal chords to tighten. However, Mother Alice, who walked slowly, would always ask one of us to go out and get her ice cream, right before she went on stage. "It helps me to sing," she would say. "I sing better if I have ice-cream, right before I go on."

One of use would dutifully go out and buy her a small helping of ice cream as directed. No matter, every night, Mother Alice performed her solo perfectly, sliding from low tenor to high soprano, and receiving a standing ovation at the end. Alice always attributed her vocal prowess to her willingness to do as the spirit directed her, and to eating her ice cream.

Gary, nicknamed The Bishop, or Bishop Gary, is one of the Choir's oldest members. Always a gentleman, and a true man of God, Gary leads us in prayer before each performance. On stage, he is a powerhouse of energy, and when he first started touring with us, his trademark was that he would quite literally dance out of his shoes as he sang. Gary has also been known, when on tour, to jump off the highest stages. During our first performance in Lithuania, on the steps of Vilnius Town Hall, Gary was singing the final song in the set. As I watched, he was first standing on the edge of the Town Hall portico, then he was sitting on its edge, and then, still singing, he disappeared! None of us could see him for a minute, until we looked out at the audience, and saw Gary running into the crowd; he had jumped fifteen feet and landed unscathed.

Gary also has a habit of grabbing us by the shoulders, shaking us, and yelling at the top of his voice, "Praise Him!" We all take this in the spirit in which it is intended, but it unnerved Anna just a little at first, until she learned how to echo him. Now, every time that Gary grabs and shakes her, yelling "Praise Him!" Anna smiles and shouts "Ditto!" This stops Gary in his tracks, and he bursts our laughing.

Craig Stagg is another long-time member. Also known as Deacon Stagg in his church, Craig trained with the Boys Choir of Harlem, while he was in high school, and he has a wonderfully velvety tenor voice. He is also very poised on stage, and a total professional, when on tour. In our set list, he owns the song, "I Believe I Can Fly," but he is very versatile. He can sing any song we ask of him, and does a fine job of directing the Choir, on occasion. During our *Good Morning America* tribute to Michael Jackson in Times Square, Craig sang the lead on Michael's song, "Will You Be There?" since the timbre of his voice is very similar to Michael's. Afterwards, complimentary emails about the performance poured in from around the country.

One of our most consistently dynamic singers on tour is Sista B., also known as Bernice Harley. Sista B. is a very gifted gospel singer and actress, and very well known in Europe. Amazingly, she can also play the drums, and on one of our tours in Italy, when our drummer refused to play, because he had been fined for being tardy, Sista B. not only sang her song, but also played the drums for the entire show. Sista B. is a woman of God, who always travels with her favorite book, the bible, and whenever there is a long ride on the tour bus, she likes to conduct bible study. If there are new people on the tour, Sitsa B. will take them under her wing, and give them guidance and counsel to smooth the way for them as they travel. She is one of our most loyal and trusted members, and is loved by the Choir, as well as by audiences around the world, that she touches with her joyous spirit.

One of the Choir's most amazing stories and inspirational characters is Sister Tamika, who sings with us on Sundays at the B.B. King Blues Club gospel brunch. Every Sunday, Tamika uses her formidable voice to give her testimony to the audience, as she sings the song, "Man from Galilee." I first found Tamika outside the club, on Forty-second Street, strung out on crack cocaine. She approached me, as I walked into the club, asking if she could join the Choir. I put her off a few times, because it was obvious that she was in no condition to perform with us. "We're having church inside," I told her. "So, if you can leave what you are doing out on the street, you can come and join us."

"I'm not ready to give that up," she replied.

A couple of weeks passed, and Tamika approached me again, asking if she could audition. "You know, Mr. Bailey," she said, "I told the Devil that I am taking back my life."

"What do you mean?" I said. She repeated what she had said: "I told the Devil that I am taking back my life."

That was several years ago, and by then, the state had already taken Tamika's three children away from her. But on Mother's Day, 2007, she arrived at B.B. King's with her children in tow. She had trod a faithful gospel path sufficiently well, not only to remain in the Choir, but also to prove to the state that she was once again a fit mother.

All three of Tamika's children have spent many Sundays listening to the Choir at B.B. King's. Her daughter Denise, who is a little lady, and our poster girl, stands on stage, and holds up the check we had made up to show our latest donation of $10,000 to Feed the Children; Tamika's younger son, Tyrique, loves to sneak on stage to play the drums after the show. And last year, Tamika's oldest Son, Dasean, came up to me. "You know what, Mr. Bailey?" he said beaming. "I just got my acceptance into Yale University."

I tell this story every Sunday that I am at B.B.'s and the audience goes wild. After the show, they come up to Dasean, if he is there, and not in church, to congratulate him and Tamika. It is always inspiring to see how with faith and perseverance a person can triumph. Tamika managed to grab hold of the lifeline that singing gospel, every Sunday in a respected venue, provided. Now every Sunday, she sings about the power of Jesus in the song, "Man from Galilee, Do You Know Him?"

Tamika's story is special and invariably moves audience members. I recently received this email:

Mr. Bailey,

I was at B.B. King's Blues Club this past Sunday. While the performance itself was outstanding, the testimony of the woman with the three children was what really moved me. I am a social worker in foster care and adoption. It was powerful for me to hear of her success in getting her children back, and then giving them such extraordinary opportunities. Often, in my line of work, we have little hope that the children will be reunified with their families, let alone have successful outcomes. It's important that we hear these messages that can provide us with more hope, as we work with these children and families. Thank you so much for the ministry you do with individuals, families and the world.

God bless,
Rachel C.

Sadly, one of our earliest and best-loved choir members is no longer with us. Samuel Joseph grew up in the same Lincoln Projects that I did, and I recruited him in 1995, from my church in Harlem, the Greater Refuge Temple. Just like my own mother, Samuel Joseph's mother was a lifelong member of the congregation there, too. The family had seven children, and, just like my father, Samuel Joseph Sr. was an able-bodied man, who, at one time, earned too little to support his family, and had to leave the home, so that they could qualify for government housing and welfare support.

From the time that he was a small child, Samuel Joseph Jr. did what he could to better himself and to help others. He started working, as a little kid, bagging groceries and doing a paper route, and if there was any way to make an extra buck to help out at home, he was there to do it.

Samuel Joseph Sr. eventually found work as a cop in Harlem, and was an officer for over fifteen years. He told me a lot of bone-chilling stories about how he had intimidated and beat up gang members, junkies and drug dealers to force them out of the community. He violated a lot of people's civil rights, but he justified it, because he said that these people were dirty and that they had it coming; it was what he and his colleagues had to do to clean up the community. He told me that he could tell just by looking at a guy, by his appearance and his manner, whether he was dirty or not. He was a cop who waved around his firearm a good deal, and he wasn't afraid to use it.

"Don't you worry about killing innocent people?" I asked him one time.

"Sometimes innocent people do get killed," he said. "Comes with doing the job. You can't worry about it." Samuel Joseph Sr. was a tough guy, and the people in the community feared him for the rough street justice that he and his cohorts dished out. I think eventually that he and a number of colleagues were discharged from the force because of abuse charges. At home, this man could also be angry and abusive to his wife and children, especially when he drank. I think Samuel Joseph Jr. loved his father, but also feared him.

I remember that Samuel Joseph often did the rounds of the dry cleaners in Harlem to ask if he could take unclaimed garments for the poor and homeless. It's not uncommon in Harlem for people, who are strapped for cash, to abandon clothes at the cleaners. I also saw him working at local carnivals, running the rides or selling cotton candy. He would work a twelve-hour shift, and often donate the money he had made to the church. Samuel Joseph had an almost painful sense of justice and social conscience. There were a lot of local gangs that he could have run with, but he was never tempted.

Samuel Joseph had a good voice, and like many gospel singers, he was round and hearty. "Can you see your feet over you belly?" Choir members would tease him. "At least I'm lucky enough to have a belly," was his answer. He was good natured and quick to laugh, but at some point, I began to notice that he was dropping a lot of weight. When I questioned him about it, he made the excuse that he was on a more healthy diet and watching his weight. But it soon became obvious that this was not true. As the months went by, he began to look sick and emaciated. I tried to get him to talk about it, but he wouldn't. Whatever was happening with him, he wanted to keep it private.

One day, I got word that he was in Harlem Hospital, and being treated for AIDS. As his illness progressed, I wanted to visit him, but he sent word that he didn't want me to see him in the condition he was, so he passed away in 1998, without my being able to visit and say goodbye. I believe he is buried in Ferncliff Cemetery in Westchester. Many famous people are laid to rest there, including Malcolm X, Betty Shabazz, Judy Garland, Jerome Kern and, of course, my mother. She died in 1963, while I was still in college, so she too is in Ferncliff, among very good company.

It's often on my mind to call Samuel Joseph's sister to find out exactly where his grave is, so that I can go up there and lay some flowers. He was a kind soul and a terrific role model for the rest of the Choir. He always gave to others, and he never wanted anything from being in the Choir, other than to develop his performance skills.

Eighteen

The Power of Gospel Music

"The Choir was fabulous last night. Everyone who attended got a blessing from the performance."
—Sharon, Arkansas

If you study great African-American performers, including Aretha Franklin, Patti LaBelle, Stevie Wonder, Whitney Houston and the Winans, to name just a few, you will discover that many of them got their start singing gospel in church. Gospel music has been handed down, in a long tradition, dating back to the times of slavery.

In years past, suffering Negros expressed their struggle through music. Blues music often reflects the black man's longing and pain, while gospel music expresses the power of faith, hope and joy to raise black folks up, and to keep them going. Through the power of the gospel, translated into song, an oppressed people managed to endure, singing of the happy day when the Lord would deliver them from suffering. When I think about this, I am often reminded of something that my mother used to say: "Black folks can't afford to go psychiatrists, so we just go to church and sing."

Gospel music, in all its forms, is known and loved worldwide. We find that the three countries with the greatest appetite for the classic gospel that the Harlem Gospel Choir performs are Japan, Italy and Ireland. We tour in these three countries constantly, and I am always astonished and touched by how many of these overseas audiences return to our concerts, year after year. Our singing transcends cultural and language barriers as audience members, who have memorized the words, belt out our songs.

In twenty-three years of the Choir's existence, any number of singers have come and gone. I have loved them all like family, and each one has added his or her own unique flavor and touch to the Choir. Some singers came from happy homes, others from broken ones; some were born into desperate circumstances, others were fortunate enough to lead easier lives. Without exception, every performer, selected to be in the Choir, has been blessed with God-given talent: a powerful voice capable of stirring audiences, and creating, as Pope John Paul II once remarked, a unique feeling or experience that goes beyond the music.

I would love to have room in this book to tell you about all the sisters and brothers who have blessed the Choir over the years. I can tell you that the unique collection of singers and musicians that make up the Harlem Gospel Choir, at any given time, do have the power to change people's lives for the better. I know this as a fact and I say it with pride.

In the scrapbook of my memory, there are stories, too many to recount, of people, both civilians and troops, whom we have met through our USO (United Service Organization) tours, and through our regular performing, who have shared with us, how much the Choir brought peace, healing or joy to their lives.

It is a great privilege to be invited by the USO to travel overseas to entertain our troops. Over the years, it has been so moving to look into the faces of young men and women in the South Korean DMZ, or in war-torn Beirut, Sarajevo and Kosovo, especially, as I remind myself that there is always the possibility that some of these kids might not be returning home. There is one song that we always perform for our armed forces called "Perfect Praise." It is a song of praise to God, and it always brings comfort and tears to the eyes of the men and women in our audience.

We have so many memorable anecdotes from our USO tours. One U.S. military bases we visited was on the island of Crete, in the Mediterranean Sea, where the electricity kept going out at the most inconvenient times. We had checked into our hotel, and I had just begun to unpack, when a choir member knocked on my door to tell me that our keyboard player, Hugh, was stuck in the elevator, because the electricity had gone out. Naturally, Hugh was upset, especially since no one could say when the electricity would come back on. Not to mention that we had a show to do later on that day.

As I have already shared, growing up in the projects had taught me how to deal with broken elevators. On this particular tour, my room was on the top floor of the hotel, so when I learned of Hugh's plight, I walked down the corridor, pried the elevator doors open, leaned into the shaft, and grabbed hold of the rope attached to the elevator pulley. I knew that if I could get it to move, all I had to do was bring it up a little bit, so that the elevator cab was level with the next floor. Then, we would be able to open the doors, and let Hugh out. Now this might not be the smartest thing that I have ever done, but it worked, and brought a smile to the faces of the Choir when Hugh announced how I had rescued him. "That's it," I told them all later at dinner, "from now on, we take the stairs. If any of you get stuck in the elevator, I will not be climbing into the elevator shaft to get you out."

Some of the bases we visit are located in out-of-the-way places, like Guantánamo Bay in Cuba, where enemy combatants were held. I remember getting off the plane at Gitmo, and being terrified, because the bats there resembled crawling, walking, flying rats.

Another time, we were invited to tour a submarine, and shown all the instruments that guide the sub during its voyage. Several of the officers on the sub told us how they manufacture their own parts to replace anything that might break. It was fascinating to see how everything, down to the smallest nuts and bolts, are all made, right there, on the submarine. Sometimes, the crew is out, in no-man's land, or water, when something gives out. The needed part shows up on the computer screen, and the order is then sent down to the head mechanic, who makes it, and hands it to the team charged with doing the repairs.

I was very impressed to see how women, on these ships and submarines, are in charge of very intricate equipment, including radar systems. I also noticed that many wear shirts decorated with multiple stars, which usually indicates that they are career navy women, who reenlist, over and over, because they love the lifestyle. I came across a young lady, who said that she was third-generation navy; her grandmother and mother were both career navy, too. She was from Hawaii, she said, where it is common for islanders to enlist.

It was a major learning experience to see how the armed forces have come such a long way in recognizing the ability of women. I enjoyed talking to all the newly enlisted people, but mostly, I enjoyed the women, because they are performing "men's work" so skillfully. I saw them doing strenuous work, and lifting heavy objects, with as much strength as their male colleagues; it was clear that they are equal to any task.

I think my most memorable experience, with the USO and the navy, was the opportunity I had to steer a ship. I only went five to ten knots and I kept asking how to use the brakes. I guess it was a dumb question, because one sailor gave me a funny look, but I was proud to take the wheel and steer the vessel.

Afterwards, we were invited into the captain's quarters for dinner, and got to experience how well fed many sailors are. The food was so spectacular that I understood why so many reenlist, not that I noticed any chubby folks. I guess their work calls for them to stay trim and they all certainly looked like they were in great shape. I saw why, when our tour of the vessel took us past a large, impressive workout area, where the crew takes physical exercise every day. The ship was always spick and span, and I learned that, despite holding thousands of navy personnel, the rooms are checked thoroughly every day.

Of course, it's impossible to think about the USO without remembering Bob Hope, and all the wonderful things he did for our troops in the armed forces, all over the world. I think that in their downtime, all entertainers should volunteer to go on tour to meet and encourage these fine young men and women, or even just visit and sign autographs. I have mentioned this idea to the Commodores, and to Kareem, to whet their appetite for a USO tour.

I encourage you too to do everything you can for these wonderful Americans, who are willing to give their lives to protect all of us and our country's interests, around the world. Don't be cynical and jaded and leave it up to others to do. Find some way, big or small, to thank them.

Anna and I continually receive letters and emails from fans, who have enjoyed a particular performance, and feel moved to write. Just recently, we received an email from an audience member who had attended a performance at B.B. King's in New York City. "Before my mother passed away," he wrote, "I brought her to your concert to celebrate what turned out to be her last birthday."

It just so happened that out that of all the people in the audience that night, I selected this young man's mother to come up on stage to sing, "O Happy Day," with the Choir. His mom was so thrilled that she spent the next whole year talking about it, about how, after being a fan for so many years, she had been on stage with the world-famous Harlem Gospel Choir. The son went on to write that he wanted to pay the Choir's expenses to fly out to Sausalito, California, to sing at his mother's life celebration.

Receiving a message like this always makes me teary eyed. I sometimes get grief from the Choir for insisting that we bring audience members on the stage; some of them tell me it's too corny, and they roll their eyes, but the opportunity to join in means a great deal to our audiences. You just never know how deeply it can affect and gladden a person, like this young man's mother, who saw the chance to sing with us as the fulfillment of an important wish.

Years ago, when I found myself touring with a young band that Benny was promoting, called the Four Kingsmen, someone, who was working with me, advised me never to go into business for myself, because, he said, I cared too much about people, and what they thought about me. He was right, and what he said still holds true today, but happily, this trait didn't prevent me from founding the Choir.

I can still remember this guy's exact words to me, out on Martha's Vineyard, where we were working at the time. "You get too involved with people, and spend too much time listening to their problems," he said, "even though it's not called for in your job description."

"You're right," I replied, "but's that's what I was brought up to do." My mother was a devoted church volunteer who was happy to take in the various waifs and strays I brought home during my tenure at Job Corps, despite the fact that she was poor, and had five sons of her own to raise.

Both my mom and dad instilled in me the belief that I would not feel good unless, and until, I gave back. "You can't just take, that will make you miserable," my mother told me. "You have to give back. People will care about you, if you show them, first, that you care about them."

Wherever we are in the world, I challenge the Choir to look with kindness and respect upon the people and cultures we are visiting. It is true that, as

African-Americans, we do have to battle some pretty negative stereotypes, at home and abroad, from people who don't even know us, but it is also true that we receive warm receptions from people who stand on line, in all kinds of weather, to buy tickets to our shows.

One warm welcome that especially stands out from many in my mind, came the time that we were booked at the Cork Opera House, in Ireland. It is an intimate theater with a gorgeous old, red interior. On this occasion, as we walked out on stage, and before we even sang a note, the audience erupted in cheers and screams. What a welcome! And it is the same every year that we return.

The Choir is immensely popular in Ireland, where the Irish love religious music in general, and our flavor of gospel music in particular. We have enjoyed touring with the Irish group, the Chieftains, and I find that there is a strong connection between the Choir and this talented band of musicians. Maybe it is the kinship of two oppressed peoples, from two opposite sides of the Atlantic, who have channeled their struggle, their passion and their hopes into music.

It is a great feeling to know that so many fans love and care about the Harlem Gospel Choir, and appreciate all that we are doing for children's charities, and for children in general. During most shows, I have developed a little routine: I bring out soft toys, usually stuffed baby elephants, that sport our Kente colors, and we give them to the little girls that we call up on stage. I tell these girls that they are special and are little Harlem Gospel Choir angels. "If you ever come up to Harlem," I say, "you have to bring this elephant with you, or they won't let you in."

Parents from all over the world email me, and sometimes send photos, showing how these little girls cherish the gift. They carry their elephants around, sleeping or snuggling with them in the car. One child christened her elephant Henry, and made the family go back home to fetch him, after they set out on a trip without the toy. Each time I bring a child on stage, I tell her, "Who you are is a gift from God, and what you make of yourself, is your gift to God."

At all of our shows, we raise money for Feed the Children and other charities, by selling our Kente-colored silicone wrist bands; each one is embossed with "Harlem Gospel Choir, God Bless the Children." This is a unique and practical way to support a charity while we are on tour, since the wrist bands are very light, and don't require a mountain of luggage. Once, as a gentleman handed me five dollars for the bracelet he had picked up, he told me to make sure that his money did not go to support the children of Afghanistan or Iraq, because these kids would, no doubt, grow up to be little Saddam Husseins and future Taliban leaders. He wanted to be certain that his money was reserved for what he called, "our children."

"Our goal is to feed all the children of the world," I answered. "We are unconcerned with their nationalities." The man put the bracelet back and turned to walk way. "Please take one free of charge," I called after him.

It often seems that there is a plan for our musical ministry, and often we learn of this plan, almost by accident. For example, after our show in Dunedin, New Zealand, Anna received an email from a man who called himself David, which read:

> *I attended your concert in Dunedin last night. I have been very angry for many years. When I arrived at the theatre, I hated God. When I left, after listening to your choir, I felt at peace for the first time in years. I intend to go back to church and to ask God to come into my life.*
>
> *Thank you,*
> *David*

Anna was excited, and read the email to the Choir the next day, after they had boarded the tour bus. Not only does the Choir give hope and inspiration, they need to receive it, too, and this email made our day.

The day before, we had flown to Dunedin from Auckland, in a very small plane. We were approaching the Dunedin runway for landing, when the plane began to roll and dip, buffeted by strong winds, coming down from the New Zealand Alps. The crew did its best to prepare us, checking that we all had our seat belts fastened, and as the plane began its final approach to the runway, it began rolling from side to side, quite violently.

Anna, who was sitting next to one of the sopranos, really wanted to look out the window at the spectacular scenery, but the girl next to her began to scream, sinking back in her seat, with her legs, climbing up the back of the seat in front of her. She continued screaming, even after the plane had landed safely. "We are going to die! We are going to die!" she kept yelling. "Darlene, we have landed," Anna repeated calmly. "We are okay. The plane has landed and everything is all right." And it did appear that we had survived the scary landing for a very good reason: God had a plan for us, and for David.

After our next tour of Australia, three years later, Anna received another email, this time from a family that had attended our concert in Caloundra. This concert was only the second stop on the tour, and some of the kinks in the show were still being worked out. We did not think this particular night's performance one of our best, by any means, and Caloundra is a small town, so we were surprised that our presenter had decided to include it on the tour. But God works in mysterious ways, as the email that Anna received, proves. We were definitely in Caloundra for a reason:

> "I just wish to thank you all from the bottom of my heart, for allowing God's spirit to re-enter my daughter's life. We were honored to see your choir perform at Caloundra, Australia, in November. As a family, we had been going through very emotional times with Bree, our fifteen-year-old daughter. She saw no purpose in life, and had been struggling with depression for some months. Life was getting way too hard for her, and she tried to harm herself, resulting in a hospital stay. As a parent, I felt devastated, but on the day of your concert, the hospital assured me that Bree was well enough to leave for a couple of days leave. I wasn't sure but, this was when the miracles started to take place.
>
> We had booked our tickets a week prior to Bree's hospital admission, and I know, now, that God especially wanted her to be present at your concert. I watched in amazement as Bree was filled with spirit until it was overflowing. I have never witnessed anything quite so amazing. Bree had lots and lots of tears, but they were tears of joy, hope, and peace. Even now, I get very emotional thinking about the whole experience. She hugged every one of the Choir, and they all filled her with God's love. I just stood back and watched it all unfold

in front of me.

After leaving the concert, Bree needed to put her feet in the sand, so we headed to the beach, keeping in mind, it was now 10PM. She sat on the sand and sang and sang, right from the bottom of her soul, and I cried and cried, right from the bottom of my soul! Emotions were coming up, from the darkest and deepest place; it was uncontrollable, but so cleansing. When we got up to leave, we noticed that her jeans had imprinted a picture in the sand. Bree was absolutely amazed, as right before her eyes, was a beautiful angel, Bree's very own sand angel! She wrote her name above her special angel, and from that moment on I knew that a greater force was with her, and that her journey to be healed had now begun. I was filled with such faith and belief in this miracle.

It is so true that when you feel there is no hope at all, and you are at your lowest, that God steps in and lifts you higher than you could ever imagine! For this, I will forever be truly grateful to you all for being present, and for being messengers from God! Thank you, thank you, thank you! We have been truly blessed. Bree is back, but she is a very different Bree; this miracle has changed her precious life forever. Keep up your wonderful work. We listen to your CD with such passion. Hope to hear you all again on your next visit to Australia.

God Bless,
Donna

It is always encouraging to hear that a performance has transcended a language barrier, and to see that the spirit in the music has touched our audience in a profound way. An example of the power of the music is highlighted by the following email that we received, after our first performance in Moscow, Russia, in 2006. We were the first gospel choir from Harlem to travel to Russia, and responses, like this, from the audience, made dealing with an extremely harsh Russian winter, very worthwhile. We are now considering the possibility of singing "Amazing Grace" in Russian, during our tour to St. Petersburg, later this year!

Hello Dear Choir

My name is Elena and I am from Moscow, from Russia. I go to Moscow Bible Church. Today I was SO VERY RICHLY blessed by getting to know you and being at the concert. You are great and awesome, though the most awesome is our Lord Jesus! You can feel His presence in the building. Thanks a lot for what you all do, and may God bless you in your ministry to others, to the nations and to the children.

I was amazed how willingly the people in Moscow, who need God, (and who doesn't?) were ready to worship Him, together with you, and through you, the Holy Spirit moved their hearts actively! I would say that it would be great the next time you come (and you promised to…), for you to sing a verse of one of the songs in Russian. In the churches all over Russia we sing some of your songs. "Amazing Grace" is, of course, the best-known, as well as, "Soon," and very soon, "O Happy Day," "This Little Light of Mine," "He's Got the Whole World" and others. And there is the translation, if you might want to have it, I may send the words to you, and would be very willing to help you learn a verse, just in case you need it.

With love in Jesus and prayers for you and your ministry.

Lena

One of the most heartening emails came in recently, after our performance in Seaside Park, Bridgeport, Connecticut, at the Festival of the Vibes. It was a dreary Sunday morning, and we had had to get up early to drive to the venue. As it was a festival, we were not the only act scheduled that day, and we had to wait to go on with no sound check. We were not happy with the sound, and felt that it compromised our performance. This feeling that the show was not quite what it should be persisted, even though the people did come out of their tents to watch, which made the organizers very happy. Something magical happened that morning, nevertheless, because we received the following email:

Dear Mr. Bailey,

I wanted to thank the Choir for their performance at the Vibes yesterday. The group inspired everyone present. I was especially thankful this year. My husband would not go with me to see the gospel singers at last year's Vibes. This year, he not only went, but he stayed and listened to the music, and truly enjoyed it. I have been praying for his salvation for a long time, and this was the closest he's been to church in 20 years. It was a real blessing! Thank you for the work that you do, and for being a mighty witness for Christ.

Yours,
Lorynda

I close with a piece of recognition that comes from the mother of one of our favorite fans in Ireland, Brian Cussen. Here is what his mom wrote:

Dear Mr. Bailey,

for many years now, I have attended your concert when it comes to Cork City, Ireland. I am the mother of four young children, ages nine, seven five and two. I have always found your concerts joyous and uplifting, and I look forward to them every year. My son Brian, who is seven, has a rare genetic syndrome, and struggles daily with things that his brother and sisters take for granted. He is so brave.
This year I have promised to take Brian and his older brother, Kevin, to your concert in Cork Opera House, on December 4th, and they are really looking forward to it. Keep up the good work.

Sincerely,
Mrs. Grace Cussen

Nineteen

On the Road Again

"I was picked out of the crowd to be sung to and that was an awesome experience. It felt like Jesus was right there. Bless you for traveling all that way."
—**Libby, Australia**

Performers, be they athletes or entertainers, are gypsies, who must take their show on the road to any place that their audience may be, from the jungles of Zaire to the stadiums of Japan. It is a source of great pride to me that the Harlem Gospel Choir enjoys an almost universal appeal, and that, although we are a ministry for Christ, we are equally committed to the spirit of Dr. King's vision of bringing nations and people together, and giving something back. These are the principles upon which the Harlem Gospel Choir was founded.

During our shows, I come up on stage, and remind our audiences that the Choir is primarily a ministry that ministers through our music. I explain to them that, for the next couple of hours, our venue will be transformed into church, and that they will become a congregation, welcomed and encouraged to join their brothers and sisters on stage, in praising the Lord. I do this in a lighthearted way, because the truth is that we want people of all faiths to feel at home at our concerts, and to experience the power of our inspirational music, and they do.

The Harlem Gospel Choir has played, and been accepted, in every venue imaginable, performing for audiences of all faiths and creeds. As the Choir sings, people seem to experience more of their shared humanity with their brothers and sisters, and fewer of their differences.

First and foremost, we are a touring choir, and there was a time when traveling was fun, but in recent years, you can't imagine the stress that we encounter at airports. Some years, we travel in the range of 200,000 miles, with up to three different choir groups circling the globe, working domestically and internationally. Fortunately, we are blessed to have wonderful tour managers who make sure that all Choir members are protected and looked after.

These tour mangers are the heart and soul of the organization, because they ensure that Choir members are always on time, dressed correctly, and conducting themselves in a professional manner at all times. The tour managers also act as counselors, when members become upset and emotional, because they are homesick or physically sick, or perhaps, because they have received a call, telling them that there are problems back home. We find ourselves in faraway places, like New Zealand or Hong Kong, and it is just not possible to hop on a plane, because someone back home is having a difficult time.

For these reasons, then, the tour manager is very important, an extension of Anna and me. Anna and I are constantly having to split up, with her going in one direction with one group, and me going in the opposite direction with another group of singers. This grueling tour schedule means that we have not spent a single Christmas together in the last ten years.

The tour managers, who support us, are our surrogates, whom we value and trust immensely. For many years, Anna and I had a rule: if one of us cannot be on a tour, then the tour will not happen. The few times in the past that we had sent out a group, under the management of someone other than ourselves, invariably there were problems—poor reviews or damaged relationships with promoters. Because relationships with agents and promoters are carefully cultivated and valued partnerships, the loss of any promoter or agent is a huge blow to us, and to the future of the Choir.

It is only recently, because the Choir is in such demand, with as many as four tours scheduled at one time, that we have found the faith to trust new personnel. It seems that the more the Choir grows in popularity, the more we are able to attract well-intentioned and talented tour managers.

Our first priority when touring is safety. Every tour is carefully prepared in advance. We examine the tour itinerary, and will even refuse tours, if they are in regions that we consider unsafe for our people. For example, we have, over the past three years, received offers to perform in Israel, and we would very much like to go there. But, in light of the current political climate in the Middle East, and in Israel, in particular, with sometimes daily reports of rockets, suicide bombs and missile fire, we have decided, in each case, to decline these offers. We feel that we cannot guarantee the safety of our personnel under those conditions, and more to the point, neither can anybody else.

In contrast, we were comfortable sending the Choir to what were formerly war-torn Bosnia, Lebanon and Kosovo. In each of these instances, the Choir's safety was guaranteed by the U.S. government, and by the U.S. military, and we were confident that, if there was any imminent danger, the Choir would be taken out of the situation immediately. In fact, the first time that the Choir went to Kosovo, it was, at one point, scheduled to perform high in the mountains. On the day that the group was due to drive to the military base, however, a recommencement of hostilities in the region forced the U.S. Army to evacuate the Choir from the region.

Before any tour departure, we spend time double-checking the hotels, the neighborhood, and the general environment of the venue we are scheduled to play. Transportation is also a priority, and we require a very special bus that can accommodate bathroom breaks and is comfortable over long distances.

The technical rider in our contract spells out the amenities we need on the bus: DVD players, music and personal TVs, which are very common requirements for musicians. The tour industry keeps transportation up-to-date, because if they don't provide the best in facilities to satisfy the needs of performers, some of whom have sizable egos, then the word spreads quickly. As a result, most of the buses we travel in have luxury kitchens and bathrooms, and facilities that can sleep fifteen people. This is critical, because we often do not have time, between stops, to rest up in a hotel. We might leave a show at eleven or twelve o'clock at night, and then have to drive eight or nine hours to our next venue for an early show, the next day.

We select our bus drivers very carefully, because they become our constant companions, and have to be able to tolerate high-voltage singing. Working with our group does come with consolations, however, as one of our regular drivers, here in the United States, points out. He enjoys dealing with our performers, because they don't use drugs or profanity, and are totally respectful of themselves, of others, and of the job that they are doing. I am always impressed with the bus drivers who drive all night to get us to a venue safely, and then stay with us, until everything is secured. We form a close bond with these people, spending as many as two or three months at a time in their company.

When I am on tour with the Choir, it is my habit to invite all of them to have dinner with me as my guests, because they are part of my family on the road, as well as my family in Christ. I like to establish an atmosphere of team spirit and cooperation on the tour from the get-go, because there is nothing worse than being on an unhappy tour for one week, one month or three months.

I always try to secure a private compartment on the bus for myself, so that I can get away from the noise, and focus on business matters. I also often stay up into the early hours of the morning, keeping my eye on things, and keeping the driver company. I want him to know that I have his back and can support him if he needs to stop or take a break.

But getting back to the torment of the airports. What I have learned, during these troubled times, is that airports have installed security men, who supposedly have been trained to recognize terrorists, just by looking into their faces. I think these individuals are called TSA men. I had a talk with one in San Francisco, who claimed that he can decide, just from people's expressions, whether or not they are carrying something illegal. "You can tell, just by looking at them, when something isn't right," he told me. This made me laugh, because it seems that no matter where I travel, I always look wrong to someone.

Going through security with me is a real trial, because I'm always the one who is asked to step to the side, and to go to the back. Without fail, I am pulled over and directed to a side room for questioning. Once, as I passed through security, an officer asked, "Who do you work for?"

"I work for Jesus," I told him.

"This guy works for Jesus," the security officer shouted to his friend. They both took note of the embroidered messages on my Harlem Gospel Choir hat and jacket. My hat said, "God has been good to me," while my jacket announced, "Exercise your faith and walk for Jesus." Anyway, I think that these officers may have logged me in the computer, because now, whenever I go through an airport, my name seems to be flagged.

One day, I asked a supervisor why I was always taken to another room to be searched, and for the usual interrogation: "Where are you going? Why are you going?" The supervisor examined my passport. "All these entries are probably what make the red flags go up," she said.

A few years back, I was put through the usual drill, when a security employee looked agitated, after seeing my name come up on a "special" list. "Am I the poster child for terrorists?" I asked in frustration, "because, without fail, you guys pull me over and interrogate me. What criteria do I fit that you always have to stop me?" The officer looked at me. "You are tall and you are black, so…you know," he said, shrugging. Sadly, I think there are plenty of "tall black men" who share my experience, and it goes beyond racial profiling.

As you can imagine, I quickly rack up frequent flyer miles, and it is not uncommon for me to upgrade my airline tickets to first-class, but this move only tends to hurt my situation. I see the questioning looks on some of the crew's faces. Why is this man traveling first class? Why does he have so many stamps on his passport from all around the world? I recently learned that there is now a special pre-screen card you can buy that allows you to just walk on through security, in a special line, for pre-approved, frequent flyers. You had better believe that I am planning to get one.

Once I am on a plane, I typically choose an aisle seat, because I have to get up and down a good deal to check on Choir members, and I hate to disturb people. One time, I was seated next to a very well-dressed lady, who was extremely fidgety. As the plane took off, we hit some turbulence. "Aw shucks!" she kept saying. Finally, I turned to her. "Are you all right?" I asked. "Do you need any help?"

"I just asked the Lord to take me," she said.

"Do you mind waiting until we land before you do that?' I said, laughing. I could write an entire book just about my experiences in airports and airplanes.

The Choir and I often feel like we live on planes, and, as you can imagine, we run into endless delays. It would be easy to spend half our lives bellyaching about delayed flights, and being stuck on a runway, when we are longing to get home, but what's the point? Needless to say, everyone in our group has great pipes, so why not put them to good use? I can't tell you how many times, I have pushed the Choir to burst into song, as our plane idles on the tarmac. It's great for morale—the other passengers', the crew's and ours. The Choir sings off their frustration, and the plane is treated to a free concert—win-win. So the next time you are delayed on the runway, you might get lucky enough to be held up in the company of the Harlem Gospel Choir, and if you are, I can guarantee that our rendition of "O Happy Day" will be sure to make your day, no matter how bad the delay.

I do try to instill in Choir members, the importance of carrying themselves in a very dignified way, when we are out in public. Unfortunately, many people around the world have heard so many negative things about black people, especially black people from the "infamous" Harlem. When we travel, it's not uncommon for people to automatically move away from us.

Once, I flew Qantas airlines to Sydney, Australia, where I was fortunate enough to check into a suite of rooms at my hotel. It was tricky getting the door to the suite open, so I asked a hotel employee for help. "This floor is for VIPs only," she said.

"Do you think that the people downstairs gave me this room key by mistake?" I asked her. She shot me a look, turned abruptly, and walked away, seemingly fuming that I was on the VIP floor.

This behavior is what I call subtle racism. I have friends in Harlem who kid me that I am a big shot now. "Come and watch me try to get a cab and then tell me how big time you think I am," I tell them. "Most cabs would sooner run me over than pick me up."

Sometimes it happens that, while I am driving a nice car with my white wife beside me, certain police officers will pull us over, request to see my documents, and then ask Anna if everything is all right. It is clear that they think I have hijacked the car and kidnapped the woman. The smarter cops just wave us on when they see Anna sitting in the passenger seat.

It is a terrible feeling to have someone judge you simply by the color of your skin. You would think in this day and age, when people are more educated, that bigoted attitudes would be waning, but I can attest that this form of subtle racism is alive and well. My prayer is that, in the coming era of President Barack Obama, much of this will go away.

I encourage Choir members on tour to react with patience, when they are on the receiving end of this kind of treatment, and to be pleasant in general, whenever they encounter hostility, or grumpy behavior, from service personnel. For example, once, when Anna and I were on tour with the Choir in the United Kingdom, we had to take a flight in a very small plane, from the Isle of Jersey to the Isle of Guernsey, in the Channel Islands.

The plane was so small that our luggage had to go on a separate flight, and we were seated on the plane, according to our weight, so that the weight would be evenly distributed. As we waited to board the plane, we saw the ground crew handling our luggage in a really rough manner. They were standing on the bags and throwing them, from one luggage cart to another, on the tarmac.

One of our tenors was very upset at seeing his luggage treated in such a way, so he yelled at the offending baggage handler. When we landed in Guernsey, we waited for the plane with the luggage to arrive and searched the carousel for our bags, but they were not there. The next plane was not until the next day, and we had to perform our show, wearing only the clothes we had with us. Fortunately, most of the Choir are experienced travelers, who know enough to pack their performance gear in their carry-on luggage. The show went off without a hitch, but the tenor, who had lost his cool, learned a very valuable lesson about how not to speak to service personnel. The lesson was reinforced by the comments he received from the rest of the Choir, who had to make do that night with no toiletries, and with no change of clothes, as we waited for our luggage to arrive the next day.

I smile at people in the face of their mistrust or annoyance. One time, I double-parked for a minute, while Anna ran a quick errand. Sure enough, the ticket maid came over immediately, and wrote me up. "I know, just doing your job," I said, smiling. I know that these people take heat all day just for doing their work. She appreciated my attitude and let me go with a caution. Then there was the token collector, on one of the New York bridges, who looked perpetually annoyed, but who could blame her? Collecting tolls is a tough gig. I went out of my way to be nice to her. "You look so pretty today," I would tell her. "That's why these tolls are getting so high, they're paying models to collect them." Then the grumpy toll-collector would lighten up; made my day, turning that frown into a smile.

"Treat people well," I tell the Choir, "because nobody forgets a bad turn, and, as my father used to say, 'If you insult a person, you also insult the ten friends they tell about it.'"

Another challenge of being on tour is the constant flack I get from the Choir because they hate wearing the "uniform." I have a rule that, whenever we travel, everyone must wear at least one piece of Harlem Gospel Choir clothing that incorporates our special Kente colors. It proudly tells the world who we are, and helps keep the work alive by promoting our ministry. In these days of high airport security, and the constant threat of terrorist attack, this rule is even more important than ever.

I constantly explain to new Choir members that they must stay with the group, while in the airport, and, if they need to leave the group for any reason, then they must tell somebody where they are going. Terrorists do not travel in groups, terrorists travel alone, so it is not likely that a terrorist would be traveling in a group of people wearing Harlem Gospel Choir garb—tour jackets, hats and bags embroidered with our logo.

Once, on tour in Portugal, our keyboard player disappeared at the airport, as we were waiting for our plane back to New York, and facing a three-hour delay. He had decided that he was too cool to wear a Harlem Gospel Choir jacket and cap, so instead, he opted for sunglasses, and his favorite hip-hop hat and do-rag. It was after we had gone through security to wait in the transit lounge that we noticed he was no longer with the group. None of us knew where he was and he was not answering his cell phone. In fact, he did not rejoin the group, until we were all on the plane. When he did finally arrive, we learned that, because he had gone through security on his own, and not with the group, and was wearing sunglasses inside the airport, he had been pulled over by airport police, subjected to a full body search, and held incommunicado, while Interpol checked his passport details. After this incident, I had less difficulty keeping the group together, and in appropriate HGC "uniform," at airports.

Keeping so many young men and women on schedule and on track is work, but after twenty-three years, I have seen it all before. I know what to expect, so I seldom get angry. I have heard every excuse for tardiness under the sun, many of them extremely creative. "Watch The Apprentice show on TV," I recently remarked to some culprits, "and let me know what you think

Mr. Donald Trump would tell you, if you were to show up chronically late for him!"

Touring with the Choir is a wonderful gift and always promises a wealth of experiences. However, when a group of people are traveling together, out of their own comfortable environment, and for any length of time, the normal stresses and strains of travel, and the resulting jet lag, can affect everyone. That is why, when we audition for new singers and musicians, we look at the person first, and the voice or talent, second. After a week or so on tour, it really does not matter how well a person plays or sings, if the price you have to pay is that he or she makes your life miserable every minute of every day.

To be able to tour, for any length of time, takes a special type of person, because, while each day on tour has a structure, every day is totally different; unexpected things happen all the time. We try to keep our tours to no more than two months, because as you become more tired, your ability to handle a stressful situation diminishes, and when that happens, the tour becomes more difficult for everyone.

On tour, good things happen, inspiring things happen, sad things happen and there is drama. What makes touring something that we will always commit to is that inspirational things take place, and the mystery is that you never know when these happenings are going to occur.

On tour for the first time in New Zealand, we traveled down to the southeast tip of the South Island, to a town called Dunedin. Dunedin is an important town in New Zealand, but to us, it felt like we had reached the end of the earth. Anna still laughs at this memory, and says that she looks forward to flying to Dunedin again, one day.

Because we try to journey, where no other choirs from Harlem go, we sometimes encounter unusual travel conditions. I already mentioned our trip to the British Channel Islands, and the Island hopping we had to do there, flying on small planes that seat only fifteen people, which includes the pilot, but no flight attendant. On this particular tour, we had been on so many flights, already, that most of us were not really fazed by the small size of the planes. However, one of our tenors, Lawrence, who was always nervous flying, became really upset at the prospect of the tight space in the small plane, and said that he would rather take the ferry, even if he had to pay for it himself. "It's not an option," Anna told him, "and, anyway, the sea is too rough to take a ferry."

"In that case," Lawrence replied, "I would rather wait in Jersey, until you all come back in two days."

Anna explained that this was not an option either. "Do you really think that I would ask you even to get on this plane, if I thought that something bad was gong to happen?" she said. "Have faith, Lawrence."

"There is a difference between faith and stupidity," Lawrence shot back.

He agreed to get on the plane, but only after several Choir members walked him outside the terminal, and onto the tarmac, to talk to him. As it turned out, the flight was uneventful. Anna, and another Choir member, sat in the back of the plane the whole time, eating cheese and crackers, while the pilot joked with everyone, by pulling out a newspaper and pretending to read, instead of handling the controls. Lawrence was really quiet on the flight, and when we landed, Anna asked him how he was doing. "Fine," he said, "I think I passed out."

Sometimes very funny things happen on tour, although to appreciate why they are funny, you have to be there. For example, on our first tour to South America, we took only a limited number of CDs with us. It was a new market and we were unsure how big the demand for CDs would be. Anna was the tour manager, and since it was our first time in the region, the promoter, Aquiles, accompanied the Choir for the entire tour. Aquiles is a great guy, who took very good care of the Choir, translating menus for the group at roadside restaurants, and helping out with sound check every day, by translating what the sound and light needs were for the performance in each venue. The shows were sold out everywhere, which meant that the forty CDs Anna brought with her to the venue went like hot cakes, selling out fast. One night in Belo Horizonte, as the selling table was being mobbed, and the last of the CDs was sold, the promoter came up to Anna. "Let's leave, now!" he urged.

"Why?" Anna asked.

"Before they keel us!" he replied, lengthening the word "kill" with his Spanish accent.

Anna laughed, but ran backstage as directed, and began to pack up the costumes. Meanwhile, excited audience members waited around for a while, hoping that more CDs would be brought out for sale, and forcing the Choir to hole up in the dressing rooms until the crowd had left, and the coast was clear.

Aquiles has always been very kind to the Choir. He is typical of good promoters, who really pay attention to the act, in order to figure out the best way to market it, as opposed to others, who only care about how much profit they can make. Aquiles always shows the group every kindness and takes the time to try to get to know each individual member. At the end of one tour, on the night before the group flew home from Buenos Aires, he took the company to a magical tango house, and treated the Choir to a unique dinner and tango show; we still have the photo from that night.

The following year, a similar situation occurred in Concepción, Chile. The venue was sold out, and the crowd not only wanted CDs, they wanted to get really close to Choir members who were sitting at the signing table. The venue had absolutely no security, and no staff to provide crowd control, so Anna abandoned selling CDs, leaving that task to me and the promoter. She positioned herself between the crowd and the signing table, and began to push the crowd back with both hands, yelling at the top of her lungs, "Non Puhen! Non Puhen!" It shocked the crowd so much that they became more orderly, all except for one man, who was intent on trying to jump across the table to get to one of the lady sopranos. "How can I get to her?" the man screamed at Anna.

"You can't!" Anna yelled back.

The fan was so shocked by Anna's determination that he backed off. After that night, Aquiles made sure that all of our venues in South America had security, at the signing table, to provide crowd control, and to make sure that the lobby was a safe place for cash sales of merchandise.

Not all promoters are created equal, and problems often arise, when the local promoters are not up to snuff. For example, the Choir was recently on tour in Brazil, working with a promoter, who often seemed scatterbrained, to say the least. One day, as the Choir arrived at the airport in Brasília, on their way to Rio for the next concert, our tour manager, Kia, noticed that the promoter and his wife, who was accompanying him at this point, were fighting.

More concerned about the Choir than about the marital spat, Kia was busy checking everyone in for the flight, when she heard uproar erupt at the adjacent ticketing counter. The promoter had forgotten to take into account the fact that, because the group had missed their scheduled flight, they were now required to pay additional airport taxes on the new tickets. The promoter's wife, who may have invested in the tour, was furious, and stormed off, almost knocking Kia down. Not knowing enough Portuguese to direct the group through the airport, Kia signaled for everyone to stay close to the rowdy couple, as they argued their way to the gate.

Once at customs, the promoter pulled Kia aside to tell her that all Choir members would have to pay the taxes on their ticket, about twenty dollars per person. Kia knew better; the contract explicitly stated that the promoter was responsible for paying all fees and taxes. She offered to collect all the tickets so that he could pay the taxes. In a soft voice, he asked her if she would mind paying them, since his budget was already stretched. Kia pulled out her tour binder, flipped to the contract, and pointed to the section stating that the Artist was not responsible for any fees or taxes. Seeing it in writing, the promoter finally took the tickets, and began haggling, unsuccessfully, with the ticket-counter agent to try and lower the price.

Later on, as she boarded the plane, Kia passed the promoter and his wife, who were still arguing. Exhausted, she fell asleep, thinking to herself that the plane seemed to be going in circles, only to be jolted awake by a Choir member, who was telling her that the cabin crew had thrown the promoter and his wife off the plane, because of their disruptive behavior.

Now Kia was stuck, without any information on the hotel or the concert venue in Rio, and without the name of the escort, who was scheduled to meet the group, once they landed. On a stop over in São Paulo, Kia called Anna in New York. "You have a company credit card," Anna reminded her. "Use it to pay for hotel rooms, taxis, and even flights, if you have to." Money problem solved, Kia next questioned the ticketing agent to see if there was any helpful information listed on their flight itinerary—a shot in the dark, but one that paid off. There was a note, saying that the promoter's stepson would meet the group, when they landed in Rio, and give them their itinerary for the next couple of days.

The promoter could not get a flight to Rio until the next night. When

Kia finally checked the group into the hotel, and got to her own room, there was a voice mail waiting for her from an ashamed promoter. In his message, he apologized profusely, begging Kia not to tell Anna about the debacle. Too late, Anna was already fully briefed.

Another disaster, waiting to happen, is poor sound quality, which can make or break a concert. It is crucial that venue staff adhere to our technical rider, and make sure that the stage is set up correctly in time for sound check. However, more often than not on tour, the Choir will arrive at a venue for sound check, only to find that the stage is not ready for them, or worse, that the stagehands do not have a copy of the rider that is always sent out in advance to the promoter, and is part of the contract. Because of this, tour managers typically try to get to venues, ahead of time, to see how preparations are proceeding.

On a particular day in Brazil, Kia had already asked the local promoter to check with the stagehands, to make sure that everything would be ready by the time the Choir arrived. Following procedure, Kia went to the venue early, only to find that the stagehands had not even set up the monitors, let alone instruments or mics. You would think that setting up a few mics, running cables, and setting up a keyboard and small drum kit, would be child's play for these seasoned stagehands; after all, the rock band, KISS, was scheduled to perform in the very same venue, the following week. Surely they could accommodate our small ensemble. Apparently not, because, when Kia arrived, nothing was set up, and she had to spoon-feed instructions to the crew, who had not bothered to look at the rider, which had been translated into Spanish by the local promoter. Exhausted, and running thirty minutes behind schedule, Kia finally started sound check, which took forever. Once done, she begged the technicians not to move anything, and not to touch the soundboard.

That evening, when the show started, it became obvious that the sound engineer had his own idea of how the Choir should sound, and Kia was horrified. The engineer was either deaf, or in a dead spot in the house, because the Choir sounded as if it were inside a base drum. Kia spent all her time, sprinting the quarter mile to and from backstage and the auditorium, checking sound levels, and begging the engineer to turn everything down in the house. Needless to say, the audience was upset, because the show was too loud; the Choir was upset, because the sound levels on stage kept changing; and Kia was upset, because she had to spend the next hour, trying to calm everyone down. It's a basic truth, unfortunate as it may be, that a sound engineer controls the quality of a concert.

Twenty

The Flying Dutchman: André Rieu

"I saw your choir on the Colbert Report with Ambassador Young. I just wanted to say that it was moving and inspirational. Thank you for all you do."
—Jesse, Florida

One day, in May 2006, Anna came running into my office. "Allen, Allen," she said, "we just got an email from André Rieu."

"Who is André Rieu?" I asked. What can I say? Sometimes I am a little narrow in my musical tastes.

"You know, the Flying Dutchman—the famous Dutch violinist." Anna looked at me as if I were the most ignorant person on earth. "They want to have a meeting with us." She was excited and handed me an email:

> Dear Anna,
>
> Let me start by introducing myself. My name is Frans Neus and I'm the International Director for Ticketing & Special Projects of André Rieu Productions. We are preparing a concert in Radio City Music Hall, on Saturday July 29th, which we will tape for television broadcasting.
>
> We are looking to involve a gospel choir (and children's choir) in our program. Can you please contact me by email or phone, at your earliest convenience, to discuss the possible participation of your choir in this event.

We are in the States, right now, and have another concert in Radio City, next Sunday, May 21st. If you want more information about us, please visit our web site andrerieu.com

*Kind regards,
Frans Neus*

Anna ran off to answer the email, right away, and so began our year and a half collaboration with André Rieu and the Johann Strauss Orchestra. One of the great things about Anna is that she answers emails as soon as she can, which is one of the reasons that we got the opportunity to work with André. Frans later explained to us that he and André really appreciated this swift response to his email.

Anna arranged for us to see the André Rieu concert the following Sunday at Radio City Music Hall. We had fabulous center-front orchestra house seats, courtesy of Frans, who took us backstage after the concert to meet André. But backstage was so mobbed with a crowd of people waiting to see the famous violinist, that we decided not to bother him then, and went home. Anyway, Anna had already arranged a meeting at Radio City for the following day.

Arriving back at the venue the next day, we were just in time to see André, always larger than life, walking backwards, through the lobby, and talking to a TV camera. "I want," he was saying, "to have the largest limousine in New York bring the orchestra to the front door of Radio City…." And he continued walking backwards, out of the lobby, and onto Sixth Avenue, followed by the camera crew. Not wanting to interrupt the taping, Anna and I sat on the stairs leading to the lobby balcony, and waited. Eventually, Frans came to find us, and took us upstairs to one of the midsized meeting rooms.

Awaiting us there were André; his son, Pierre; his publicist, Kirsten Cornelis; and the film crew. André shook our hands and asked would we mind if the meeting were filmed. "No problem," we said and the meeting began. André explained how he would like the Choir to be part of his show at Radio City Music Hall that coming July, and how he would also like them to perform with him and the orchestra, earlier in the same month, at the

Vrijthoff Square in Maastricht, André's home town, in Holland. We found it easy to agree to most of his requests and liked the spirit of collaboration that he offered us. And so our partnership began. When we left the room, so excited at this new and promising venture, André followed us out and shook our hands, warmly flashing his famous smile, and making us feel on top of the world.

In the weeks that followed, André had his production team send us mp3's of the songs that he wanted the Choir to sing during the show, both in Maastricht, and at Radio City. He saw our collaboration as a partnership that allowed his orchestra to perform gospel songs: "O Happy Day," "Amen," "Jesus Can Work It Out" and "O When the Saints." At our meeting with him, we had explained the special choreography that we always incorporate into our shows, whenever we sing "Jesus Can Work It Out" and "O When the Saints." For the former song, we perform what we like to call the Harlem Gospel Choir Shuffle; for the latter song, we send two singers out into the audience, and start up a conga line, grabbing people from their seats and leading them around the hall, up onto the stage, and then back to their seats. André loved the idea of the dancing and audience participation, and had a special addition built in front of the stage, at Radio City, to accommodate this choreography. It was a huge success on the night.

To complete the cultural exchange on the stage, the Choir would learn songs from a nongospel repertoire: the "Hallelujah Chorus," "Amigos Para Siempre,'" the "Nun's Chorus," from the Strauss Opera *Casanova*, and "I Will Follow Him," from the movie *Sister Act*.

André wanted fifteen singers from us, but no musicians; not our usual touring format. Because of this, and the new material, we scheduled a week of intense rehearsals, in New York, before the shows in Maastricht. The Choir learned the new material in typical gospel fashion—by ear. We played those mp3s over and over again in rehearsals, and, as always, Anna burned all the files onto a CD, so that each singer could practice the songs at home, and sing them as André's choir did, ready for the next rehearsal.

Needless to say, rehearsals were stressful. Initially Anna hired a classically trained keyboardist to teach the nongospel songs, including the very difficult "Hallelujah Chorus." Unfortunately, as this gentleman began to teach the song, it became clear that he would take much longer than the time we had allotted to learn it. On top of this, he kept cautioning the Choir about how difficult it would be for them to learn the piece, so we paid him, and asked him to leave. Next, one of our own singers stepped in to teach the Choir their parts to the Chorus, as well as the other nongospel songs. With this move, things began to go much faster, with rehearsals progressing according to schedule.

Finally, the day came for the first rehearsal with André and the orchestra in Maastricht. The orchestra was rehearsing a really spectacular version of "Singing in the Rain" that André had requested for the two outdoor shows, on the stage at Vrijthoff Square, where we too would be performing.

Everyone in the orchestra was incredibly welcoming. As the Choir climbed the steps leading to the stage, and each person stepped onto the stage, the orchestra, in unison, sang "Wooo Oooooo," ending on a high inflection. One of our singers was quite large, even for a gospel singer, and, as she stepped onto the stage, she fell and almost pulled down the two people helping her. "Woo Oooooo," the orchestra sang again, but this time, they ended on a down inflection. It was really quite amusing. I remember how impressed I was, with how in-sync everyone seemed to be, right from the start.

Needless to say, the shows at Vrijthoff and Radio City Music Hall were wonderful, and André was so happy with the performance that he asked if we would allow him to put the songs, sung by the Choir, on a new CD called New York Memories, as well as on the DVD, also called New York Memories, which was shot at Radio City Music Hall. Both Anna and I were delighted, especially since the CD subsequently went on to go five times platinum in Australia, and the DVD has been shown on PBS stations in New York many times since.

André was so happy with the audience response to the collaboration between his orchestra and the Choir, that he took us on tour with him in Europe and Japan, for just over three months. The Choir loved traveling with him, because he does everything in a first-class manner, and is very generous.

Once, when the Choir had performed with the orchestra in the Gelredome in Holland, and were on their way back to Maastricht, they found themselves in a substandard hotel, late at night. Even though his liaison did all she could to rectify the situation, and drove those Choir members with the most unacceptable rooms to another nearby hotel at 2AM, André still gave each member of the Choir a gift of 150 Euros, so that they could go shopping in Maastricht, while they waited for the tour to move on to Japan. Later, each of us received a personalized note from André, communicating his apologies. That is the quintessential André—first class all the way.

Twenty-one

The Queen of Daytime TV and Rock Royalty: Oprah and Lisa Marie Presley

> *"I wanted to let you know that I love what the Choir does! You are an inspiration to me and so many people! Thanks! I grew up in the Civil Rights Movement in the '60s, in Alabama, singing on Sundays, in churches, including in an all-African-American church, where the singing left me filled with the spirit for the rest of the week. Peace and God's grace to you."*
> —**Brother Ian**

It was a phone call for which you wait a lifetime, when in September 2007, we received a call from Rachel, a producer at the Oprah show, which was celebrating its twenty-fifth anniversary on the air. Rachel explained that Oprah was planning to record a show in New York City, at Madison Square Garden, no less, and with a very special guest.

To commemorate the thirtieth anniversary of her father's passing, Lisa Marie Presley had recorded an old Elvis hit, "In the Ghetto," creating a music video that combined images of beautiful toddlers and infants, with old footage of Elvis performing the song. Lisa Marie had laid her own voice on the track. The result was very touching. It looked like Lisa Marie was singing a duet with her father, much in the same way that Natalie Cole, daughter of Nat King Cole, had set her voice to her father's classic song, "Unforgettable."

Lisa Marie's video was beautiful and a wonderful tribute to her dad.

Oprah was going to showcase the video on her show, and feature Lisa Marie singing live with the recording of her father behind her—a real tearjerker. Rachel asked me if the Harlem Gospel Choir would sing live backup behind Lisa Marie on the show. I was elated at the prospect of the Choir singing with Elvis's daughter. We would have crossed continents to do it, but we didn't even have to leave Manhattan! As she briefed us on the project, Rachel mentioned that in reading about Elvis, she had learned how many of his moves came from watching black preachers.

It was wonderful working with Oprah's professional staff, which paid perfect attention to every detail of the production. Show producers must have checked in with us at least a hundred times before the taping. "Wear black robes," one of them instructed us during a call. We explained that black robes on black skin on television would not look good, but the producer insisted. "Black robes will work best with the turquoise dress that Lisa Marie will be wearing," she said.

We showed up with the Choir on Saturday to rehearse for the show taping, which was set for two days later. Lisa Marie and her terrific husband, Michael, spent a good deal of time with the Choir. They had originally requested a hundred and fifty singers. "Where am I going to find that many singers in one week?" I asked. "Our touring choirs typically total only about twelve members each," I explained. In the end, we settled on fifty singers, which would give the performance enough drama and still be manageable for us to pull together. We tapped into our local churches to swell the Choir's numbers.

When we arrived on set for rehearsal, the producers finally saw for themselves why it was not a good idea to dress the Choir in black robes. "Can you get white robes?" one producer asked Anna, who shook her head. "Tomorrow is Sunday, and I can't get my hands on fifty sets of white robes before the performance on Monday," she said.

Well, Oprah's influence is certainly considerable, because, when the Choir showed up on Monday to rehearse before the show, white robes were waiting. Producers had knocked on doors around the city to beg and borrow the garments. The effort was worth it, because word came back that Lisa Marie was very happy with how things looked, so problem solved.

We had been asked to arrive at final rehearsal by 5:50AM for makeup, blocking, and a run through with Lisa Marie and the orchestra. You can imagine how gospel singers sound so early in the morning, so we had to order plenty of tea with honey and lemon.

We had the chance to meet Riley, Lisa Marie's grown daughter, who is a beautiful young lady. It is easy to see the resemblance to Elvis in his daughter and granddaughter—the same shape face and beautiful eyes; it is a very good-looking family.

Lisa Marie thought the Choir was exceptional and wanted a photo session with us, and it pleased us to no end to spend that time with her. And it was a great privilege to be part of the twenty-fifth anniversary of Oprah's show.

Before show time, I was standing backstage, waiting for the rest of the Choir to arrive, when I saw Ms. Winfrey jump out of a black SUV. She nodded and dashed into the building. I have to say that Oprah did seem larger than life, as she leapt from that SUV and hurried into Madison Square Garden, as lines of her fans wrapped around the block, hoping to catch site of her, or secure a seat to the show. Later on, Oprah acknowledged me and thanked us for our work.

That day, I also had the opportunity to meet David Letterman. He was a scheduled guest, and was very funny, telling jokes backstage. How fortunate I am to be here, I told myself, with these talented people, and with the opportunity to have the Choir's performance beamed around the world to millions.

This time, it was Anna's turn to miss out on a huge event. The day of the broadcast, she was flying with another choir group, to Maastricht, Holland, to begin a tour with André Rieu. There was no time for her to attend the filming, as she had to leave for JFK Airport in the middle of the day, and she had had no time to pack over the weekend. So Anna watched the show, as it aired on TV in the business-class lounge, courtesy of André. Naturally, she was very happy, and called me to tell me how fabulous everyone looked and sounded in the final take.

Oprah and Lisa Marie could have asked any choir to participate in this historic taping, but they blessed us by choosing ours; it was a very proud moment. Afterward, Oprah's producers called to thank us, and to tell us that the show was such a hit with the audience, they were sure that the episode would be rerun due to popular request. As for us, we enjoyed every minute of the experience, and have nothing but high praise for the staff of Oprah's HARPO Productions.

Twenty-two

Lifting up the World with a Oneness Heart: Sri Chinmoy

"Tatiana works in Sweden as a Hospital Theological Care Worker and came to New York for a vacation with her brother. Her work is emotionally draining. Your concert was like 'spiritual food' for both of us. When it ended, I had a wonderful peaceful feeling; all my troubles had vanished."
—Marie, Brooklyn, New York

Back in 1998, Natabara Rollason, one of the disciples of the famous spiritual and fitness guru, Sri Chinmoy, contacted us by email. Natabara explained that he worked at the United Nations, and lived in Jamaica, Queens, near Sri's Ashram. Sri Chinmoy's goal, he explained, was to promote world peace. Natabara went on to ask if the Choir would allow Sri Chinmoy to include them in a series of weightlifting events called "Lifting Up the World with a Oneness Heart." From either a standing or a seated position, Sri Chinmoy would attempt to lift the Choir, using a counter-balance beam. He had already held a series of these events around the world. I think he had even lifted an airplane—and now he wanted to lift the Harlem Gospel Choir! I was amazed and honored.

Sri Chinmoy was very gracious and charming, always smiling, and in remarkably good physical shape for a man in his late sixties. Apparently, his disciples were all long-distance runners, who ran every day as part of their spiritual practice. Sri Chinmoy himself could no longer run, due to a knee injury, but he told me that he had resumed a program of physical fitness, as part of his spiritual meditation, and that, since he could not run, he was attempting to lift weights that no man, not even a much younger man, could lift. He was doing this, he said, to demonstrate the power of the spiritual over the physical. "A man can do anything," he told me, "if he possesses a 'Oneness Heart'."

Sri Chinmoy loved the Choir, especially one of our ex-members, Sean, who sang with us at that time. I remember that he would always hold Sean's hand for a little longer than anyone else's, as he greeted each member in turn, on the stage, before the event began.

Sri Chinmoy told me that he did not think any faith or spiritual path was superior to any other, and you could tell that he truly believed this by how warmly he greeted the Choir members. He completely understood the principles of Dr. Martin Luther King, on which I had founded the Choir. He said he believed that Martin was, at once, "the bravest child of divinity, and the dearest brother of humanity." He went on to say that Dr. King was "the embodiment and revelation of a dream, that sleeplessly and breathlessly cried for the manifestation of a oneness heart, here in America." And that he was, indeed, "a hero-supreme of this earth planet." It truly touched my heart to hear these words from someone born in Bangladesh, who was not a Southern Baptist, but of the Hindu faith, and who could still so deeply appreciate what Dr. King meant to me.

The photo of me with Sri Chinmoy, along with the medal that each Choir member and I received, after the lifting event, are still two of my treasured possessions. The Choir participated in two "Lifting Up the Choir with a Oneness Heart" events. Both were held in Queens, in the auditoriums of local schools.

At the first event, the Choir was on a long, cantilevered beam, high off the ground, and Sri Chinmoy stood underneath them in a kind of cage-like structure, as he lifted their combined weight. While the lift was not huge, in terms of inches, it was truly amazing, because it could not have been achieved without complete body and mind concentration. After all, our choir members are not noted dieters! After the lift, Sri Chinmoy joined the Choir on the stage, while they sang gospel songs in his honor.

The second lift was also held at a school in Queens, and this time, there was even more excitement, because by now, people realized how much Sri Chinmoy liked the Choir. Each of us, including Anna, was individually weighed, and then we all climbed up the steps and onto the beam. Fortunately, it had a railing that we could hold, so none of us were in danger of falling. This time, Sri Chinmoy lifted from both a standing and a seated position. Our combined weight was well over 1,500 pounds, and the measurements of how high we were lifted, were recorded in hundredths of an inch. Everyone was very happy. Sri Chinmoy then invited the Choir to stay, while he performed some of his new compositions on the auditorium stage.

In January 1999, I organized our annual Martin Luther King Day concert at the Players Club in Gramercy Park, New York. I have belonged to the club for many years and was, in fact, the first black member to be accepted. That year, we performed our usual set in honor of Dr. King, and then we sang the song that Sri Chinmoy had written especially for the Choir. Some of his followers came to the club that night, and took photos of the performance, so that he could see them, as he was not able to be there in person.

From time to time, after he lifted the Choir, Sri Chinmoy would invite Anna and me, as VIP guests, to his concerts in Manhattan. I can remember him sitting there in a beautiful round chair on the stage, with various Indian instruments on the floor beside him. His most devout followers were dressed in wonderfully colorful Indian garb, and seated in the front rows near us. On the stage, there was a choir of women followers in lovely saris.

As Sri Chinmoy closed his eyes and began to play, I remember that the atmosphere in the room was very warm and expectant. All eyes and ears were attuned to the guru. But, while both Anna and I really appreciated the kindness and the warm welcome, and the fact that the best seats were reserved for us, I found it very hard to sit still for so long, listening to music that was so different from gospel, and from any music that I knew.

Anna told me that the music was a stream of consciousness, and that the guru's followers believed it came from divine inspiration. While my mind could appreciate this amazing claim, my legs and back could not, and all too soon, I would have to stand up, and walk, as quietly as possible, out of the room, with Anna following behind me.

Anna did not like having to leave those VIP seats early, especially in full view of all of the guru's followers, and I think that Sri Chinmoy did not appreciate our early departure. He may have thought that it was disrespectful of us, and perhaps he was right. I do know that, after the second occasion, we received no more VIP invitations to his concerts.

Twenty-three

Two Popes and Two Presidents

"Last week I saw your choir perform at Pope Benedict's mass in Yankee Stadium. Your singing really conveyed the joy of the occasion."
—Isabel, New York City

I end, almost as I began, by remarking on what an honor it was, as well as a highlight, in both my own and in the Choir's career, to sing for President Obama, at the Apollo Theater in Harlem, back in February, 2008, when he was still a senator and running for the Democratic Party nomination. Other performances, that have matched this one in significance, are those that took place when we were called upon to sing for three other outstanding political and spiritual leaders: Nelson Mandela, former president of South Africa, Pope Benedict XVI and the beloved Pope John Paul II.

To perform just once for a pope is a great honor; to perform for a pope three times, can only be viewed as a great gift from God. The Choir sang once for Pope Benedict XVI, and twice for his predecessor, Pope John Paul II. I believe that Pope John Paul II particularly enjoyed the Choir's performances, because, some years later, Anna was in New York, chatting with Monsignor Franco, who had spent many years working for Pope John Paul II at the Vatican, when the monsignor told her how much the late pope had loved the Choir.

After one performance, the pope had remarked that the Choir does more than sing. "They create a special feeling or experience," he had said. This was rewarding to hear, but not news to us, aware, as we are, that when great gospel singers perform, they are literally filled with spirit, which, in turn, fills and touches the audience in a way that no other music can.

Besides enjoying our music, I believe that the pope also appreciated the work that we do for children's charities around the world. Pope John Paul

II was, himself, a tireless advocate for children, and a passionate admirer of Mother Teresa, and the work that she did, and that her Sisters of Mercy still do, on behalf of the orphans of Calcutta.

When Pope John Paul II's successor, Pope Benedict XVI, made his first visit, as pope, to New York to pray for peace at ground zero, and to celebrate a televised mass before a crowd of almost 60,000 in Yankee Stadium, the Choir was invited to sing at the pre-mass Concert of Hope. As a prelude to the celebrations, a local TV show, *Good Day New York*, on Fox 5, invited the Choir to sing in-studio.

I could not be part of the excitement in New York. I was on tour with another group of singers from the Choir. On the same day as the Concert of Hope in New York, my group was scheduled to sing the National Anthem at Chase Field, prior to the Arizona Diamondbacks game against the San Diego Padres.

Anna, therefore, was organizing the group of eighteen singers and two musicians, who would perform at Yankee Stadium as part of the Concert of Hope. On Saturday, the day before the concert, Anna met the singers and our tour manager, Henry, for a sound check at the stadium. It was essential that Henry be there, because, the following day, while I was in Arizona, Anna would be at B.B. King's with yet another arm of the Choir, and Henry would be responsible for the group at Yankee Stadium.

Tickets for the concert could not be purchased and were a very hot commodity. Every local Catholic church had only a limited number of tickets to distribute to its congregation, via a lottery. The Choir was performing gratis, but we did arrange for every singer to have a seat in the bleachers, so that they could attend the mass after the concert.

The Choir would sing two songs on their own: "O Happy Day" and "Amazing Grace," and two songs with Stephanie Mills: "Never Knew Love Like This Before" and "We Can Move Mountains." They were to be accompanied by their keyboard player and drummer, who would be situated in the orchestra pit with the Harry Connick Jr. Orchestra. This arrangement meant that the singers would not be able to see the musicians, and the musicians would have a very limited view of the Choir, since the orchestra pit was forty feet in front of the stage, and there would be several rows of VIP seating between the musicians and the stage. Communication, between the singers and musicians, would be almost impossible, during a performance in front of 60,000 people, that would be broadcast live to millions of people around the world. Naturally, everyone was very nervous.

That Saturday, while everyone waited in a tent across the road from the stadium, the Choir rehearsed their songs, and consumed the sandwiches, sodas and water that had been provided. Anna suggested that, while they waited for sound check, it would be a great opportunity for them to rehearse with Ms. Mills, but this did not happen.

After more than two hours of waiting, the Choir was shepherded across the stadium to wait on benches in the corridor, where so many famous baseball players had waited over the years. Finally, the Choir was directed to walk up the stairs, over the boards that had been carefully laid on the grass, and up the wooden ramp to the stage, already resplendent with the papal seal and throne.

The lead singers for "Amazing Grace" were handed wireless mics, as the Choir grouped around the corded mics on stands. The sound check began, but after the first lead singer had sung only a few bars, the Choir was told that they were out of time. Anna was annoyed and the Choir was insulted. They had arrived on time, and waited patiently for over two hours, only to have their sound check cut ridiculously short. This meant that they would have to sing in front of countless people without having had a proper sound check. Anna looked straight at the stage manager. "Unbelievable!" she exclaimed, as she walked back down the ramp.

Later that day, Anna received an apology email from the stage manager, who explained that the preceding sound checks had taken far too long, that the orchestra, which had been there all day, had to leave by 5PM, and that the stadium crew had run out of time to complete the remaining sound checks.

The next day, with Allen in Arizona, Anna at B.B. King's, and Henry at Yankee Stadium, the sun shone brightly, and everything went according to plan. The show at B.B. King's had been rescheduled to start at 11:00AM, instead of the usual 1:30PM, to accommodate an early load-in by another artist set to perform later that day. This meant that while Anna could not be at the stadium for the Choir's performance, she could go home in time to watch it on TV. She still talks about how the Fox 5 commentator declared that he had never heard such a wonderful rendition of "Amazing Grace."

The Choir received a standing ovation, and this dynamic performance set a high bar for Kim Burrell and Harry Connick Jr. who had to follow them.

It seems that Anna is destined to be blessed with papal contact. In December of 2003, she was in Italy with one group of the Choir, while I was on tour in Japan with another group. In Italy, the Choir was to perform at Sala Nervi, the 12,000-seat concert hall at the Vatican, along with other performers from around the world. As a bonus, two members of the Choir had been cleared to join a small group that would meet Pope John Paul II for an audience, a couple of days before the concert.

Rehearsals for the performance were spaced over two days, and as is so often the case with such complicated events, there was a good deal of waiting around and eating at local ristorantes close to the Vatican. On the second day of rehearsals, a car pulled up to the hotel to take the two lucky Choir members to the Vatican, for the audience with Pope John Paul II. Anna rode with them to make sure that everything was all right.

Inside the Vatican, when the group of people, assigned to meet the pope, was directed to begin walking, Anna walked with them, and to her surprise, no one stopped her. The group followed the path leading to the back of Saint Peter's Basilica, past beautiful buildings, and through ornately manicured gardens, until they came to the doorway of the building where the meeting with Pope John Paul II was to take place. Next, the group began to climb the winding Renaissance stone stairway, until it reached a magnificent room with red and gilt walls, and small golden chairs, set in very straight rows.

Because the Choir members with Anna were both heavier and slower than the rest of the attendees, they were the last to enter, and took the only remaining seats at the back of the room; this turned out to be a blessing. Suddenly, the doors at the rear of the room opened. A Choir member, scrambling to find the camera in her purse, almost caused the security team, standing at the side of the room, to tackle her. As Anna stood, and turned around, she found herself, face to face, with Pope John Paul II, as he was wheeled towards her, into the room. That day, the best seats were at the back of the room.

The pope, who was in poor health, addressed the group, speaking softly in Italian, thanking all the performers in the room for contributing to this annual concert, which raised funds for the Five Churches of Rome. Next, each row was called up to meet the pope. The photo that Anna had taken of her holding his hand, is one of her treasured possessions.

It always seems curious to me, how often we have received unexpected and unlooked-for blessings, simply by being ready to go with the flow, to grab an opportunity, and to act with faith. It certainly does seem that sometimes God has a plan, and all we have to do is ask and follow.

On the night of the concert, there was another unexpected event, that brought everyone involved into the worldwide spotlight. American singer, Lauryn Hill, was a scheduled performer at the concert. The Choir noticed on the day that she was very aloof, and took far too long to sound check her solo. That evening's concert was wonderful, and the front seats were occupied with the cardinals of Rome in their red and purple cassocks.

All was well until Lauryn took the stage. She stood at the mic, and launched an attack on the Catholic Church, based on the recent pedophile scandal involving priests in the United States. "I'm not here to celebrate, like you, the birth of Christ, but to ask why are you not in mourning for his death in this place?" Lauryn read from a prepared statement, going on to blast the Church, and to accuse them of moral corruption. A few audience members clapped, unaware of what Lauryn was saying, and then she began to sing. Most of the audience, including the Choir, looked on, in stunned silence, as she performed her song, and then marched off the stage. Some of the cardinals walked out in protest. That night Lauryn Hill embodied everything that the Choir is not: rude, ungrateful, insulting to her hosts, and willing to use her talent to push a political agenda.

The April 2007, pre-mass Concert of Hope for Pope Benedict XVI took place at Yankee Stadium. Seventeen years earlier, when the Choir was still in its infancy, it had performed in that same venue for another great man—Nelson Mandela, who had been touring the United States, and was in the stadium to lead a rally against apartheid in his homeland of South Africa.

As Mandela took the stage, on that June evening, at close to 10PM, the stadium crowd, at least 80,000 strong, was chanting, "Amandla! Amandla!" a Zulu word, meaning "power," that everyone mistakenly thought meant "freedom." No matter, the chanting crowd created a huge surge of energy to accompany Mr. Mandela's dramatic presentation.

In his fight for freedom, this courageous man had endured twenty-seven years of incarceration in tiny cells, in South African prisons, refusing to trade off his political and social convictions to win his release. Once liberated, he would go on, with the African National Congress party, not only to end apartheid, but also to become, in 1996, the first president elected in his country, in a fully democratic and representative multiracial election.

On that June night, in New York, he mesmerized the massive crowd with his powerful message: "Death to racism!" His words echoed around the stadium, located right there on 125th Street, so close to Harlem, where our own Civil Rights Movement had flourished.

Mr. Mandela closed his address with special words for the people, who had so warmly welcomed him: "The people of New York," he said, "we admire you, we respect you and, above all, we love you." When New York's then Mayor, David Dinkins, placed a Yankee jacket around the leader's shoulders, Mandela smiled. "You now know who I am?" Mandela said. "I am a Yankee."

This inspirational event was part of a tour organized by Harry Belafonte. Before the stadium rally, there had been an emotional church service in Harlem, and after the service, Mr. Mandela had taken a walk, ending up at the intersection of streets, named for Dr. Martin Luther King Jr. and Adam Clayton Powell Jr. The sidewalks were jammed with people, as Mandela planted a tree there with soil that he had carried from Soweto. As the excited crowd chanted "Viva Mandela! Viva Mandela!" he told them that African-Americans and black South Africans shared a special relationship, and were connected by an umbilical cord.

"My only regret," Mandela said, "is that I am unable to embrace each and every one of you." Then he told the people how he and the African National Congress had been following the struggle of blacks in Harlem for thirty years.

Mr. Mandela's visit was very powerful and uplifting for all of us in Harlem. Obviously, he was a personal hero of mine; the parallels between President Mandela, as he was to become, and Dr. King are obvious. Both men were inspired by Gandhi, and his commitment to nonviolent resistance that he had used to win freedom for India from the British.

I was deeply gratified that the Choir was selected to perform for the African leader, and I enjoyed a private exchange with the great man. "I did not know," I told him, "that you knew and liked the Harlem Gospel Choir." Mr. Mandela pinned me with his penetrating brown eyes. "Well, you are here, aren't you?" he said, with a serious face, and in his deep, powerful voice. We certainly were there, and it was yet another great blessing in a lifetime filled with many.

Twenty-Four

Sundays at Home in New York

"Harlem Gospel Choir, thanks so much! I really needed a dose of the Holy Ghost. God bless you and your ministry. Your sister in Christ!"
—Maria Muldaur

Since the Choir is faith-based, rather than Church-based, for a long time, we were without a permanent home. Our musicians and vocalists come from many different churches in Harlem, and now that our ministry has become so popular, we have spread our net farther afield. These days, we work with talented people from the Bronx, Queens, Brooklyn, New Jersey, Rhode Island, Massachusetts and Pennsylvania, and occasionally, from as far away as Florida and Georgia. We conduct several tours to Europe and Asia each winter, and we sing at local events all year round, but it is only recently that we have found a home, where we can perform each week. And it is not a church! It is B.B. King Blues Club, on West Forty-second Street, in the heart of Times Square.

There is quite a saga behind our becoming established in such an unlikely venue, because not only is the club not a religious house of worship, it did not even exist when the choir first began its ministry. So, becoming a fixture at B.B. King Blues Club was not something that we aspired to or planned.

Every week, a million people walk past B.B. King's, which is owned and operated by the Bensusan family, which also owns the famous Blue Note Jazz Club in Greenwich Village, and the Blue Note Jazz clubs in Japan and Italy. Many years ago, Steve Bensusan had approached me to suggest that the

Choir perform at the Greenwich Village Blue Note. I remember that this was in 1999, just after John F. Kennedy Jr. was killed in his light aircraft, along with his wife and sister in law. This opportunity represented a step in a new direction for us, with the chance to perform for both a local and a tourist audience in a prestigious venue. We were all very excited, and accepted the invitation eagerly, forgetting that the Blue Note is a small club with a tiny stage, half of which is occupied by a grand piano and a set of drums. Nevertheless, we somehow managed to fit three musicians and nine singers on the stage, and across the floor in front of the stage, and we performed two sets to sold-out audiences. We were happy, the audience was happy and the club was happy.

By that time, the Choir was already a fixture at the Blue Note Jazz Clubs in Japan, where we discovered just how much the Japanese people love gospel music. Our shows were so successful that the Osaka Blue Note started a school for gospel music, based in part on our repertoire, and on the enthusiasm that we had generated among Japanese audiences.

Anna and I were gratified to have world-wide recognition, and we were welcome in so many countries, but we still had no permanent home. We constantly talked about how much a permanent home would mean to the Choir, and how wonderful it would be to have a venue in New York, where we could perform every week. It was one of our constant prayers.

And then, one day in February 2001, Steve Bensusan called again. They had opened the B.B. King Blues Club at 237 West Forty-second Street the prior year. The area was being cleaned up and gentrified by the Times Square Consortium of local businesses; Disney had taken over the Amsterdam Theatre, and the porn shops had all been relocated farther west, off Forty-second Street. This meant that now both tourists and locals were much more comfortable walking around the Times Square area, during the day, and at night.

The new club, which has a wonderfully intimate and comfortable main room, was doing well with its evening shows, but was not drawing people to the Sunday brunch, which featured a small jazz combo. Steve wanted to know if the Choir would be available every Sunday for a gospel brunch.

As so often happens, such momentous events seem to take place without me, and this time was no different, as I was away on tour. It was February, and I was with one group of the Choir on a DoD (Department of Defense) tour to Korea and Japan. So Anna went alone to meet with the then club manager. He was very happy about the new arrangement, because it meant that he would not have to worry about booking the resident artist each Sunday. Instead, it would be Anna's job to book the personnel, to make sure they showed up, and that the performance began on time. And Anna was only too happy to agree to all his demands, because, if the brunches were a success, the Choir would have the home that we had dreamed and prayed about.

Our first brunch at B.B. King Blues Club was on Sunday, February 25, 2001, and we had, by our current standards, a small audience of just over 150 people. But the club management was happy, because this represented a huge increase in attendance, and in revenue for the Sunday Brunch.

The club was not used to featuring gospel music, and still today, we are the only gospel choir that performs at B.B.'s, as we affectionately call the club. Since, in a way, we were a new cultural experience for the club, we took a big interest in how the brunch was run, working closely with the marketing department to ensure an authentic gospel/church experience for the audience. We even invited the marketing manager to come with us to experience the gospel brunch buffet at the Cotton Club, and to see how everyone in the audience could be fed soul food, in a traditional and efficient manner. Since that time, with a few changes in chefs, the soul-food buffet brunch has become an institution at B.B.'s. Now it is also duplicated for their Saturday Beatles Tribute brunch that is performed by Strawberry Fields. I wonder what John Lennon would think of that!

We have been at B.B.'s for almost nine years now. We have never missed a performance, and continue to sell out shows regularly, even in depressed economic times. Anna and I still get a thrill from seeing the Choir's name on the marquee outside the club every Sunday, and on the front marquee, during the week. Although the club's capacity is too small for the brunch to be considered a Broadway show, we feel that with a resident Disney show (first *The Lion King* and now *Mary Poppins*) across the street, we are in very good company indeed. Neither Anna, nor I, ever miss a brunch show if we are in town, and we still look forward to every Sunday, even though it means that, effectively, we never get a day off.

The managers and servers at B.B.'s have embraced us wholeheartedly. The servers wear a black shirt with a Kente tie as part of their uniform, so that, by extension, they are a part of the show, and since we are often sold out, and we encourage the patrons to leave a tip, the servers compete with each other for a spot on the brunch. They are a very talented, supportive and efficient crew, and it is a delight to work with them each Sunday. I love to stand at the beginning of the buffet line, and direct the patrons to the two sides of each buffet station; a very necessary job, when the show is sold out, if the performance is to begin on time. And it is a great way to meet the audience before I go on stage.

Having a permanent home at B.B.'s means that we have somewhere each week, where we can invite promoters, agents and sponsors—a wonderful blessing. It also represents steady work for the performers, many of whom are not able to be on the long domestic and international tours, but who have amazing talent, and are able to minister so effectively on stage through the music. And lastly, it means that we have a presence in our hometown, and not just out of state and internationally. We have a local following, something that very few internationally touring gospel choirs ever get to experience. It is still a wonderful feeling when an audience member comes up, either to Anna or to me, and says something like this:

Hi, do you remember me? I was here two years ago, and today, I have brought my mother for her birthday! We are so excited!

Anna and I grin from ear to ear when we hear words like these and say a silent prayer of thanks every time.

Twenty-five

Farewell to Michael Jackson

> *"Mr. Bailey, I just returned home from church today, where my family and I had the privilege to watch the HGC in person. What a wonderful experience! The Choir was magnificent, and I can't wait to see them again someday. You are doing a great job with the HGC. May God continue to bless you and the Choir"*
> —**Phillip Trujillo & Family**
> **Albuquerque, New Mexico**

Life sometimes brings you full circle. My career in the entertainment industry could be said to have begun with many things and with many people. One of these people was Michael Jackson, whom I first met on the Jackson Five tour, when the Commodores were the opening act. I think Michael was about eleven years old then, and although we had both worked with famous people before, this particular tour would impact both of our lives in a huge way.

Michael and I took paths that led us in very different directions, but like a perfect circle, life and music brought me back to Michael Jackson in July, 2009. Unfortunately, it was in a shocking and unexpected way. On Tuesday, July 7, the Harlem Gospel Choir performed in Times Square for the TV show, *Good Morning America*, as part of its coverage of Michael Jackson's memorial in Los Angeles that day.

Sadly, Michael had died of cardiac arrest the previous week, and his memorial service was to be a live bicoastal telecast. The morning of the event, the Choir was the only group, invited by the ABC network, to honor Michael with a live performance of select Michael Jackson's songs, right there in Times Square, outside the television studios. It was an incredible honor, and viewed by over twenty million people around the world.

As a result of Michael's passing, the Choir has called its upcoming, international winter tours, Concert of Hope: Remembering Michael Jackson. This will include a ground-breaking tour to China; we will be the first gospel choir from Harlem to travel there. Our touring set list will include several songs by Michael: "We Are the World," and "Will You Be There?" and "I'll Be There" by the Jackson Five. Like Michael's music, the Choir's music transcends race and brings joy to all who hear it.

No matter what we plan, and no matter what obstacles are put in our way, it seems that it is our destiny, inescapable, not of our making, and always our honor, to sing God's work.

The End